M A U D E
A D A M S

ACTING EDITION
OF

Romeo and Juliet

With Drawings by
ERNEST HASKELL AND C. ALLAN GILBERT

Published with the authorization of
CHARLES FROHMAN

𝔑𝔢𝔴 𝔜𝔬𝔯𝔨
R. H. RUSSELL
1899

The PERSONS *of the* PLAY

The cast as produced at the Empire Theatre, New York, May 8th, 1899.

ESCALUS, prince of Verona	*George Fawcett*
PARIS, a young nobleman, kinsman to the prince	*Orrin Johnson*
MONTAGUE } heads of two houses at	*W. H. Crompton*
CAPULET } variance with each other	*Eugene Jepson*
AN OLD MAN, of the Capulet family	*Frederick Spencer*
ROMEO, son of Montague	*William Faversham*
MERCUTIO, kinsman to the prince, and friend to Romeo	*James K. Hackett*
BENVOLIO, nephew to Montague, and friend to Romeo	*Jos. Francoeur*
TYBALT, nephew to Lady Capulet	*Campbell Gollan*
FRIAR LAURENCE, a Franciscan	*W. H. Thompson*
FRIAR JOHN, of the same order	*Geo. Osborne, Jr.*
BALTHAZAR, servant to Romeo	*G. H. Howard*
SAMPSON } servants to Capulet	*Wallace Jackson*
GREGORY }	*Thomas Valentine*
PETER, servant to Juliet's nurse	*R. Peyton Carter*
ABRAHAM, servant to Montague	*George Irving*
AN APOTHECARY	*Norman Campbell*
LADY CAPULET, wife to Capulet	*Miss Helen Morgan*
JULIET, daughter to Capulet	*Miss Maude Adams*
NURSE to Juliet	*Mrs. W. G. Jones*

Pages to Paris, Mercutio, Capulet, etc.; Citizens of Verona, Kinsfolk of both Houses, Maskers, Guards, Musicians and Attendants.

SCENE—Verona, Mantua. PERIOD—14th Century.

The FIRST ACT Scene 1   Verona. A public place.
                 Scene 2   Before Capulet's house.
                 Scene 3   Hall in Capulet's house
                 Scene 4   Capulet's garden.

The SECOND ACT Scene 1   Friar Laurence's cell.
                  Scene 2   A street.
                  Scene 3   Capulet's garden.

The THIRD ACT Scene 1   Friar Laurence's cell.
                 Scene 2   A street.
                 Scene 3   Friar Laurence's cell.

The FOURTH ACT Scene 1   Juliet's chamber.
                  Scene 2   Friar Laurence's cell.
                  Scene 3   Juliet's chamber.

The FIFTH ACT Scene 1   Mantua. A street.
                 Scene 2   Verona. A churchyard.
                 Scene 3   Tomb of the Capulets.

Produced under the stage direction of WILLIAM SEYMOUR.

Some of the scenes in the play which are reproduced in this book are from photographs especially taken by Sarony and Joseph Byron.

THE play as here given is the actual acting version arranged by Miss Adams, with the stage directions for its performance as produced by her.

R O M E O & J U L I E T

ACT I

SCENE I.—*Verona. A Public Place. Sunday morning. Various groups idling and gossiping. Enter* SAMPSON *and* GREGORY, *of the house of* CAPULET, *with swords and bucklers, R.U.E. through Arch, down C.*

SAMPSON.

REGORY, on my word, we'll not carry coals.

GREGORY.

No, for then we should be colliers.

SAMPSON.

[*Moving with swagger to R.*] I strike quickly, being moved.

GREGORY.

But thou art not quickly moved to strike.

SAMPSON.

[*Crossing to L.*] A dog of the house of Montague moves me.

ROMEO *and* JULIET

GREGORY.

To move is to stir, and to be valiant is to stand: therefore if thou art moved, thou runn'st away.

SAMPSON.

A dog of that house shall move me to stand.

GREGORY.

The quarrel is between our masters and us their men.

SAMPSON.

'Tis all one. I 'll show myself a tyrant!

GREGORY.

[*Looking off L.*] Draw thy tool; here comes two of the house of Montagues!

SAMPSON.

[*Drawing—turns—then retreats to R. of Gregory.*] My naked weapon is out; quarrel, I will back thee.

GREGORY.

How, turn thy back and run?

SAMPSON.

[*Drawing Gregory over to R.*] Let us take the law of our sides; let *them* begin.

GREGORY.

I will frown as I pass by, and let them take it as they list.
[*Enter* BALTHASAR *and* ABRAHAM *L. 1 E., moving up to R. C.*

SAMPSON.

Nay, as they dare. I will bite my thumb at them; which is a disgrace to them, if they bear it. [*Crosses, in front, to L. H., Gregory following him.*

ABRAHAM.

[*Stops C. and down R. C.*] Do you bite your thumb at us, sir?

SAMPSON.

I do bite my thumb, sir.

ABRAHAM.

Do you bite your thumb at us, sir?

SAMPSON.

[*Aside to Gregory.*]   Is the law of our side, if I say ay?

GREGORY.

No.

SAMPSON.

[*Stepping towards* ABRAHAM.]   No, sir, I do not bite my thumb at you, sir, but I bite my thumb, sir.   [*Moves up C.*

GREGORY.

[*Following him, stops and eyes* ABRAHAM.]   Do you quarrel, sir?

ABRAHAM.

Quarrel, sir! No, sir.   [*Crosses to L.*

SAMPSON.

[*Swings down C.*]   If you do, sir, I am for you; I serve as good a man as you.

[*Enter* BENVOLIO *R. U. E. with Two Servants.*

ABRAHAM.

No better.

SAMPSON.

Well, sir.

GREGORY.

[*Seeing* TYBALT *coming L.* 1 *E.   Aside to* SAMPSON.] Say "better"; here comes one of my master's kinsmen.

SAMPSON.

[*Crossing to* ABRAHAM.]   Yes, better, sir.

II

ABRAHAM.

You lie.

SAMPSON.

Draw, if you be men.—Gregory, remember thy swashing blow. *[They fight.*

[Enter TYBALT *L. 1. E. and three Capulet Servants who rush up and attack the two men who entered with* BENVOLIO.

BENVOLIO.

[Returning from stairs.] Part, fools!
Put up your swords; you know not what you do.
[Beats down their swords and goes up C.

TYBALT.

What, art thou drawn among these heartless hinds?
Turn thee, Benvolio, look upon thy death.

BENVOLIO.

I do but keep the peace; put up thy sword,
Or manage it to part these men with me.

TYBALT.

What, drawn, and talk of peace! I hate the word,
As I hate hell, all Montagues, and thee:
Have at thee, coward!
[They fight up C. and off R. 3 E.
[Enter Several of both Houses R. and L. H. who join the fray; enter Citizens, with clubs.

FIRST CITIZEN.

Clubs, bills, and partisans!

SECOND CITIZEN.

Strike! beat them down!

THIRD CITIZEN.

Down with the Capulets! *[All repeat the cries.*

ROMEO *and* JULIET

FOURTH CITIZEN.

Down with the Montagues!   [*A general tumult.*
[*Enter* CAPULET *R., followed by two Pages and one Servant; and enter* MONTAGUE, *Page and Servant, Page with sword which* MONTAGUE *draws L. 1 E.*

MONTAGUE.

[*Advancing on Capulet.*]   Thou villain Capulet!
                [*Re-enter* BENVOLIO; *down C.; holds* MONTAGUE.
            Hold me not, let me go.
                        [*L. U. on balcony.*
[*Enter* PRINCE *with his Train, four Servants from L. 1 E. and between the two old men (long staffs for servants). Officer and Guards on from L. 1 E., L. U. E. and R. U. E.*

PRINCE.

                    [*L. 3 E. above on balcony.*
Rebellious subjects, enemies to peace,
Profaners of this neighbor-stained steel,—
Will they not hear?   What, ho! you men, you beasts,
On pain of torture, from those bloody hands
Throw your mistemper'd weapons to the ground
And hear the sentence of your moved prince.
Three civil brawls, bred of an airy word,
By thee, old Capulet, and Montague,
Have thrice disturb'd the quiet of our streets,
And made Verona's ancient citizens
Cast by their grave beseeming ornaments,
To wield old partisans, in hands as old;
If ever you disturb our streets again,
Your lives shall pay the forfeit of the peace.
For this time, all the rest depart away!
[PRINCE *descends stairs, followed by Pages.   Crosses to C.*
You, Capulet, shall go along with me;

13

And, Montague, come you this afternoon,
To know our farther pleasure in this case,
To old Free-town, our common judgment place.
Once more, on pain of death, all men depart.

[*Trumpets sound, L. H. Pages advance and give him hat and sword.*

[*Exeunt C. L. all but* MONTAGUE *and* BENVOLIO. CAP-ULET'S *Pages follow him.* MONTAGUE'S *Page gives him cane and takes sword.*

MONTAGUE.

Who set this ancient quarrel new abroach?
Speak, nephew, were you by when it began?

BENVOLIO.

Here were the servants of your adversary
And yours close fighting ere I did approach.

MONTAGUE.

But where is Romeo? saw you him to-day?
Right glad I am he was not at this fray.

BENVOLIO.

An hour before the worshipp'd sun
Peer'd forth the golden window of the east,
A troubled mind drove me to walk abroad;
Where, underneath the grove of sycamore
That westward rooteth from the city's side,
So early walking did I see your son:
Towards him I made; but he was ware of me
And stole into the covert of the wood.

MONTAGUE.

Many a morning hath he there been seen,
With tears augmenting the fresh morning's dew;
Black and portentous must this humor prove,
Unless good counsel may the cause remove.

BENVOLIO.

My noble uncle, do you know the cause?

MONTAGUE.

I neither know it nor can learn of him.
Could we but learn from whence his sorrows grow,
We would as willingly give cure as know.

BENVOLIO.

[*Looking off R. U. E.*] See, where he comes; so please
   you, step aside;
I'll know his grievance, or be much denied.

MONTAGUE.

I would thou wert so happy by thy stay,
To hear true shrift.

           [*Exit L. 1 E. followed by Page and Servant.*

BENVOLIO.

[*Enter* ROMEO *R. U. E.*] Good morrow, cousin.

ROMEO.

Is the day so young?

BENVOLIO.

But new struck nine.

ROMEO.

Ah me! Sad hours seem long.
Was that my father that went hence so fast?

BENVOLIO.

It was. What sadness lengthens Romeo's hours?

ROMEO.

Not having that which, having, makes them short.

BENVOLIO.

In love?

ROMEO *and* JULIET

ROMEO.

Out—

BENVOLIO.

Of love?

ROMEO.

Out of her favor, where I am in love.

BENVOLIO.

Alas, that love, so gentle in his view,
Should be so tyrannous and rough in proof!

ROMEO.

Alas, that love, whose view is muffled still,
Should without eyes see pathways to his will!
Where shall we dine?—O me!   What fray was here?
Yet tell me not, for I have heard it all.
Here's much to do with hate, but more with love.
Why, then, O brawling love!   O loving hate!
O anything, of nothing first create!
O heavy lightness!   Serious vanity!
Misshapen chaos of well-seeming forms!
This love feel I, that feel no love in this.
Dost thou not laugh?

BENVOLIO.

No, coz, I rather weep.

ROMEO.

Good heart, at what?

BENVOLIO.

At thy good heart's oppression.

ROMEO.

Why, such is love's transgression.
Griefs of mine own lie heavy in my breast;

16

Which thou wilt propagate, to have it prest
With more of thine; this love, that thou hast shown,
Doth add more grief to too much of mine own.
Love is a smoke raised with the fume of sighs;
Being purged, a fire sparkling in lovers' eyes;
Being vexed, a sea nourish'd with lovers' tears;
What is it else? a madness most discreet,
A choking gall and a preserving sweet.
Farewell, my coz. [*Going R. U. E.*

BENVOLIO.

Soft! I will go along!
And if you leave me so, you do me wrong.

ROMEO.

What, shall I groan and tell thee?

BENVOLIO.

Groan! Why, no; but sadly tell me who.

ROMEO.

In sadness, cousin, I do love a woman.

BENVOLIO.

I aimed so near when I suppos'd you lov'd.

ROMEO.

A right good mark-man! And she's fair I love.

BENVOLIO.

A right fair mark, fair coz, is soonest hit.

ROMEO.

Well, in that hit you miss; she 'll not be hit
With Cupid's arrow; she hath Dian's wit,
And, in strong proof of chastity well arm'd,
From love's weak childish bow she lives unharm'd.
She hath forsworn to love; and in that vow

Do I live dead, that live to tell it now.

BENVOLIO.

Be rul'd by me; forget to think of her.

ROMEO.

O, teach me how I should forget to think.

BENVOLIO.

By giving liberty unto thine eyes;
Examine other beauties.

ROMEO.

'Tis the way
To call hers exquisite, in question more.
He that is stricken blind cannot forget
The precious treasure of his eyesight lost.
Show me a mistress that is passing fair,
What doth her beauty serve but as a note
Where I may read who pass'd that passing fair?
Farewell; thou can'st not teach me to forget.

BENVOLIO.

I'll pay that doctrine, or else die in debt.

[They retire R. 3 E.
[Enter CAPULET, *and two Pages,* PARIS *and one Page,*
and PETER, *L. U. E.*

CAPULET.

But Montague is bound as well as I,
In penalty alike; and 'tis not hard, I think,
For men so old as we to keep the peace.

PARIS.

Of honorable reckoning are you both;
And pity 'tis you liv'd at odds so long.
But now, my lord, what say you to my suit?

CAPULET.

But saying o'er what I have said before:
My child is yet a stranger in the world;
Let two more summers wither in their pride,
Ere we may think her ripe to be a bride.

PARIS.

Younger than she are happy mothers made.

CAPULET.

And too soon marr'd are those so early made.
But woo her, gentle Paris, get her heart,
My will to her consent is but a part;
This night I hold an old accustom'd feast,
Whereto I have invited many a guest
Such as I love; and you, among the store
One more, most welcome, makes my number more.—
Come, go with me.

[PARIS *goes up to his Page and sends him off R. U. E.*
[*To* PETER, *who rises, giving a paper.*

Go, sirrah, trudge about
Through fair Verona; find those persons out
Whose names are written there, and to them say
My house and welcome on their pleasure stay.

[*Exeunt* CAPULET *and* PARIS *R. 1 E., followed by two*
CAPULET *Pages.*

PETER.

Find them out whose names are written here! It is
written that the shoemaker should meddle with his yard
and the tailor with his last, the fisher with his pencil and
the painter with his nets; but I am sent to find those persons whose names are here writ, and can never find what

names the writing person hath here writ. I must to the learned.—In good time.   [*Moves to R. C.*

[ROMEO *and* BENVOLIO *come forward R. U. E thru gh Arch down L. C.*

BENVOLIO.

Tut, man, one fire burns out another's burning,
One pain is lessen'd by another's anguish;
Take thou some new infection to thy eye,
And the rank poison of the old will die.

ROMEO.

[*To* PETER, *who is bowing R.*]   God-den, good fellow.
                                  [*Crossing to* PETER *C.*

PETER.

God gi' good-den—I pray, sir, can you read?

ROMEO.

Ay, mine own fortune in my misery.

PETER.

Perhaps you have learned it without book: but I pray, can you read anything you see?

ROMEO.

Ay, if I know the letters and the language.

PETER.

Ye say honestly; rest you merry!   [*About to go up C.*

ROMEO.

Stay, fellow; I can read.   [PETER *gives scroll to* ROMEO.
                                  [*Reads.*

'Signior Martino and his wife and daughters; County Anselme and his beauteous sisters; the lady widow of Vitruvio; Signior Placentio and his lovely nieces; Mercutio and his brother Valentine; mine uncle Capulet, his wife, and

daughters; my fair niece Rosaline; Livia; Signior Valentio
and his cousin Tybalt; Lucio and the lively Helena.'
A fair assembly; whither should they come?

PETER.

Up.

ROMEO.

Whither?

PETER.

To supper; to our house.

ROMEO.

Whose house?

PETER.

My master's.

ROMEO.

Indeed, I should have ask'd you that before.

PETER.

Now I 'll tell you without asking; my master is the great
rich Capulet; and if you be not of the house of Montagues,
I pray, come and crush a cup of wine. Rest you merry!

[*Exit C. to L.*

BENVOLIO.

At this same ancient feast of Capulet's
Sups the fair Rosaline whom thou so lov'st,
With all the admired beauties of Verona.
Go thither, and with unattainted eye
Compare her face with some that I shall show,
And I will make thee think thy swan a crow.

ROMEO.

When the devout religion of mine eye
Maintains such falsehood, then turn tears to fires;
One fairer than my love! the all-seeing sun

Ne'er saw her match since first the world begun.

BENVOLIO.

Tut! you saw her fair, none else being by,
Herself pois'd with herself in either eye;
But in that crystal scales let there be weigh'd
Your lady's love against some other maid
That I will show you shining at this feast,
And she shall scant show well that now shows best.

ROMEO.

I 'll go along, no such sight to be shown,
But to rejoice in splendor of mine own.

[*Exeunt R. 3 E.*

SCENE II.—*Moonlight. Music outside (supposed to be in house.) A street adjoining* CAPULET'S *house. Sunday: at night. Enter* BENVOLIO, MERCUTIO, ROMEO, *R. 1 E. with five or six Maskers, Torch-bearers and Musicians.*

ROMEO.

[*R. H.*] What, shall this speech be spoke for our excuse?

Or shall we on without apology?

BENVOLIO.

[*R. C.*] The date is out of such prolixity.
We 'll have no Cupid hoodwink'd with a scarf;
But let them measure us by what they will,
We 'll measure them a measure, and be gone.

ROMEO.

Give me a torch; I am not for this ambling:
Being but heavy, I will bear the light.

ROMEO *and* JULIET

MERCUTIO.

[*Down C.*] Nay, gentle Romeo, we must have you dance.

ROMEO.

Not I, believe me. You have dancing shoes
With nimble soles; I have a soul of lead,
So stakes me to the ground I cannot move.

[*Sits on bench R. C.*

MERCUTIO.

You are a lover; borrow Cupid's wings,
And soar with them above a common bound.

ROMEO.

I am too sore enpierced with his shaft
To soar with his light feathers, and, so bound,
I cannot bound a pitch above dull woe;
Under love's heavy burthen do I sink.

MERCUTIO.

Give me a case to put my visage in.

[*Putting on mask that Servant hands him.*

A visor for a visor! what care I
What curious eye doth quote deformities?
Here are the beetle-brows shall blush for me.

[*A party of Guests enter L. 1 E. and Exeunt C. to L.*

BENVOLIO.

Come knock and enter; and no sooner in,
But every man betake him to his legs.

[*Crossing up, and behind, to R. C.*

ROMEO.

A torch for me!
I 'll be a candle-holder, and look on.

MERCUTIO.

Come, we burn daylight, ho.

23

ROMEO *and* JULIET

ROMEO.

Nay, that's not so.

MERCUTIO

I mean, sir, in delay.
We waste our lights in vain, like lamps by day.
Take our good meaning, for our judgment sits
Five times in that ere once in our five wits.

ROMEO.

And we mean well, in going to this mask;
But 'tis no wit to go.

MERCUTIO.

Why, may one ask?

ROMEO.

I dreamt a dream to-night.

MERCUTIO.

And so did I.

ROMEO.

Well, what was yours?

MERCUTIO.

That dreamers often lie.

ROMEO.

In bed asleep, while they do dream things true.

[BENVOLIO *gets L. H.*

MERCUTIO.

O, then, I see Queen Mab hath been with you.
She is the fairies' midwife, and she comes
In shape no bigger than an agate-stone
On the fore-finger of an alderman,
Drawn with a team of little atomies
Athwart men's noses as they lie asleep;

24

ROMEO *and* JULIET

Her wagon-spokes made of long spinners' legs,
The cover of the wings of grasshoppers,
The traces of the smallest spider's web,
The collars of the moonshine's watery beams,
Her whip of cricket's bone; the lash of film;
Her waggoner a small grey-coated gnat,
Not half so big as a round little worm
Prick'd from the lazy finger of a maid;
Her chariot is an empty hazel-nut
Made by the joiner squirrel or old grub,
Time out o' mind the fairies' coachmakers.
And in this state she gallops night by night
Through lovers' brains, and then they dream of love;
O'er courtiers' knees, that dream on court'sies straight;
O'er lawyers' fingers, who straight dream on fees;
O'er ladies' lips, who straight on kisses dream:
Sometime she gallops o'er a courtier's nose,
And then dreams he of smelling out a suit;
And sometime comes she with a tithe-pig's tail
Tickling a parson's nose as a' lies asleep,
Then dreams he of another benefice.
Sometime she driveth o'er a soldier's neck,
And then dreams he of cutting foreign throats,
Of breaches, ambuscadoes, Spanish blades,
Of healths five fathom deep; and then anon
Drums in his ear, at which he starts and wakes,
And being thus frighted swears a prayer or two
And sleeps again.   This is that very Mab——

ROMEO.

[*Rises.*]   Peace, peace, Mercutio, peace!
Thou talk'st of nothing.

[*Servant speaks to* BENVOLIO *up* C

25

ROMEO *and* JULIET

MERCUTIO.

               True, I talk of dreams,
Which are the children of an idle brain,
Begot of nothing but vain fantasy,
Which is as thin of substance as the air,
And more inconstant than the wind.

BENVOLIO.

This wind you talk of blows us from ourselves;
Supper is done, and we shall come too late.

ROMEO.

I fear, too early; for my mind misgives
Some consequence, yet hanging in the stars,
Shall bitterly begin his fearful date
With this night's revels:
But He that hath the steerage of my course
Direct my sail!—On, lusty gentlemen.

BENVOLIO.

Strike, drum.

    [*Exeunt C. to L., followed by Servants and Musicians.*

SCENE III.—*A room in* CAPULET's *house.* *Sunday.* SAMP-
    SON, PETER *and other Servants discovered.* *Enter*
    GREGORY *L. 2 E.*

GREGORY.

Where's Potpan, that he helps not to take away? He
shift a trencher! he scrape a trencher!

PETER.

When good manners shall lie all in one or two men's
hands, and they unwashed, too, 'tis a foul thing.

26

ROMEO *and* JULIET

GREGORY.

Away with the joint stools, remove the court cupboard. [SAMPSON *and Servants do so off R. U. E.*] Look to the plate.

PETER.

[*To Serving Man who is crossing from R. U. E. to L. 1 E.* Good thou, save me a piece of marchpane; and, as thou lovest me, let the porter let in Susan Grindstone and Nell.

GREGORY.

[*Calling off R. and L.*] Antony and Potpan!

SERVING MAN.

[*Entering L. U. E.*] Ay, boy, ready.   [*Down C.*

GREGORY.

You are looked for and called for, asked for and sought for, in the great chamber.   [*Crossing to L. and exit L. 1 E.* We cannot be here, and there, too.

[*Exit L. 1 E. followed by other Servants.* Cheerly, boys; be brisk awhile, and the longer liver take all.   [*Exit R. U. E.*

[*Enter* LADY CAPULET *and* NURSE *L. 1 E.*

LADY CAPULET.

Nurse, where's my daughter? Call her forth to me.

[*Crosses to window R. 1 E.*

NURSE.

I bade her come.—What, lamb! what, [*Calling off L. 1 E.*] lady-bird!—

God forbid!   Where's this girl?   What, Juliet!

[*Calling upstairs R.*

JULIET.

[*From Garden L. U. E. within.*] How now!   Who calls?

27

ROMEO *and* JULIET

[LADY CAPULET *turns from window.*

NURSE.

Your mother.

JULIET.

[*Entering R. U. E.*]　　　　Madam, I am here.
What is your will?

LADY CAPULET.

[*Coming to* JULIET.]　This is the matter: Nurse, give
leave awhile.　　　　　　　　[NURSE *turns away.*
We must talk in secret.　Nurse, come back again.
　　　　　　　　　　　　　　[NURSE *returns.*
I have remembered me, thou 's hear our counsel.
Thou know'st my daughter 's of a pretty age.
　　　　　　　　　　　　　[*Sitting on dais R.*

NURSE.

Faith, I can tell her age unto an hour.

LADY CAPULET.

She 's not sixteen.

NURSE.

　　　　　　　How long is it now
To Lammas-tide?

LADY CAPULET.

　　　　　　　A fortnight and odd days.

NURSE.

Even or odd, of all days in the year,
Come Lammas-eve at night shall she be sixteen.
Susan and she—God rest all Christian souls!—
Were of an age.　Well, Susan is with God;
She was too good for me:—but, as I said,
On Lammas-eve at night shall she be sixteen;

28

ROMEO *and* JULIET

'Tis since the earthquake now eleven years,
My lord and you were then at Mantua;
Nay, I do bear a brain—but, as I said——

LADY CAPULET.

Enough of this! I pray thee hold thy peace.

NURSE.

Peace, I have done! God mark thee to his grace!
Thou wast the prettiest babe that e'er I nurs'd;
An I might live to see thee married once,
I have my wish.   [*Moves away a little.*

LADY CAPULET.

Marry, that "marry" is the very theme
I came to talk of.—Tell me, daughter Juliet,
How stands your disposition to be married?

JULIET.

It is an honour that I dream not of.

LADY CAPULET.

Well, think of marriage now; younger than you
Here in Verona, ladies of esteem,
Are made already mothers: by my count,
I was your mother much upon these years
That you are now a maid.   Thus then in brief:
The valiant Paris seeks you for his love.

NURSE.

[*Down L. of* JULIET.] A man, young lady! lady, such
  a man,
As all the world—why, he's a man of wax.

LADY CAPULET.

Verona's summer hath not such a flower.

NURSE.

Nay, he's a flower; in faith, a very flower.

29

It is e'en so? why, then I thank you all:
I thank you, honest gentlemen; good night.
More torches here! [*Guests all exeunt.*] Come on then,
  let 's to bed. [*L. U. E.*
Ah, sirrah, by my fay, it waxes late
I 'll to my rest.

> [*Exit* LADY CAPULET, OLD CAPULET *and* CAPULET,
> *L. 1 E. Lower lights.* JULIET *and* NURSE *C., re-*
> *enter* MERCUTIO *and* BENVOLIO. ROMEO *down L. H.*

J U L I E T.

Come hither, Nurse. What is yond gentleman?

> [*Exit* BENVOLIO *L. U. E.*

N U R S E.

[*R. of her.*] The son and heir of old Tiberio.

J U L I E T.

[*R. C.*] What 's he that now is going out of door?

> [*Exit* MERCUTIO *L. U. E.*

N U R S E.

Marry, that, I think, be young Petruchio.

J U L I E T.

What 's he that fellow there, that would not dance?

> [*Exit* ROMEO *L. U. E.*

N U R S E.

I know not.

J U L I E T.

[*C.*] Go ask his name.

> [NURSE *crosses in front. Exit L. U. E.*
>   If he be married,

My grave is like to be my wedding bed.

36

Were in a mask ?

OLD CAPULET.

By 'r Lady, thirty years.

CAPULET.

What, man ! 'tis not so much,
Come Pentecost as quickly as it will,
Some five and twenty years.

OLD CAPULET.

'Tis more, 'tis more.

[CAPULET *and* OLD CAPULET *move up* L. H.

ROMEO.

[*Enter* SERVING MAN *L. 1 E., crossing to R. To a Serving Man.*
What lady is that, which doth enrich the hand
Of yonder knight ?

SERVING MAN.

I know not, sir. [*Up to* L. *of* C. *and speaks to* LADY CAPULET.
TYBALT *enters* L. U. E. *and passes, at back, to* LADY CAPULET.

ROMEO.

O, she doth teach the torches to burn bright !
It seems she hangs upon the cheek of night
Like a rich jewel in an Ethiop's ear ;
Beauty too rich for use, for earth too dear!
The measure done, I 'll watch her place of stand,
And, touching hers, make blessed my rude hand.
Did my heart love till now ? Forswear it, sight!
For I ne'er saw true beauty till this night.

[OLD CAPULET *up with* CAPULET.

ROMEO *and* JULIET

TYBALT.

[*Down L. C., followed by Serving Man.*]   This, by his voice,
   should be a Montague ;—
Fetch me my rapier, boy.   [*Servant crosses and exit L. 1 E.*
                What, dares the slave
Come hither, covered with an antic face,
To fleer and scorn at our solemnity?
Now, by the stock and honour of my kin,
To strike him dead I hold it not a sin.

CAPULET.

[*Down L. of* TYBALT.]   Why, how now, kinsman! wherefore
storm you so?

TYBALT.

Uncle, this is a Montague, our foe,
A villain that is hither come in spite,
To scorn at our solemnity this night.

CAPULET.

Young Romeo, is it?

TYBALT.

                'Tis he, that villain Romeo.

CAPULET.

Content thee, gentle coz, let him alone :
He bears him like a portly gentleman ;
And, to say truth, Verona brags of him
To be a virtuous and well-govern'd youth.
I would not for the wealth of all the town
Here in my house do him disparagement ;
Therefore, be patient, take no note of him :

It is my will, the which if thou respect,
Show a fair presence and put off these frowns,
An ill-beseeming semblance for a feast.

TYBALT.

It fits, when such a villain is a guest ;
I 'll not endure him.

CAPULET.

He shall be endur'd :
What, goodman boy! I say, he shall : go to ;
Am I the master here, or you ? Go to.

TYBALT.

Why, uncle, 'tis a shame.

CAPULET.

Go to, go to ;
You are a saucy boy :—
Be quiet or— [*Crosses to L. 1 E. and calls off.*] More light,
    more light— [*Then returns to* TYBALT.
For shame I 'll make you quiet.
—What ! [*Crosses to C. as dance finishes.*] Cheerly, my
    hearts!

TYBALT.

Patience perforce with wilful choler meeting
Makes my flesh tremble in their different greeting.
I will withdraw ; but this intrusion shall,
Now seeming sweet, convert to bitter gall.

    [*Exit L. 1 E. Every one up stage,* JULIET *at window L.*

ROMEO.

[*L. of* JULIET. *To* JULIET.] If I profane with my un-
    worthiest hand

ROMEO *and* JULIET

This holy shrine, the gentle fine is this :
My lips, two blushing pilgrims, ready stand
To smooth that rough touch with a tender kiss.

JULIET.

Good pilgrim, you do wrong your hand too much,
Which mannerly devotion shows in this ;
For saints have hands that pilgrims' hands do touch,
And palm to palm is holy palmer's kiss.

ROMEO.

Have not saints lips, and holy palmers too ?

JULIET.

Ay, pilgrim, lips that they must use in prayer.

ROMEO.

O, then, dear saint, let lips do what hands do ;
They pray, grant thou, lest faith turn to despair.

JULIET.

Saints do not move, though grant for prayers' sake.

ROMEO.

Then move not, while my prayer's effect I take.   [*Kisses her.*
Thus from my lips by thine my sin is purg'd.

JULIET.

Then have my lips the sin that they have took.

ROMEO.

Sin from my lips ?   O trespass sweetly urg'd !
Give me my sin again.

ROMEO *and* JULIET

JULIET.
You kiss by the book.

NURSE.
[*Down L. C.*] Madam, your mother craves a word with you.
[JULIET *crosses between* NURSE *and* ROMEO *and up C.*

ROMEO.
[*Stopping* NURSE, *who is about to follow* JULIET.] What is her mother?

NURSE.
Marry, bachelor,
Her mother is the lady of the house,
And a good lady, and a wise; and a virtuous.
I nurs'd her daughter, that you talked withal;
I tell you, he that can lay hold of her
Shall·have the chinks.

ROMEO.
Is she a Capulet? [NURSE *nods and up C.*
O dear account ! my life is my foe's debt.
[*Second dance begins.*

BENVOLIO.
[*Down R. of* ROMEO.] Away, begone ; the sport is at the best.

ROMEO.
Ay, so I fear; the more is my unrest. [*Up stage with* MERCUTIO *and* BENVOLIO.

CAPULET.
[*L. C. when dance over.*
Nay, gentlemen, prepare not to be gone ;
We have a trifling foolish banquet towards.

35

ROMEO *and* JULIET

It is e'en so? why, then I thank you all :
I thank you, honest gentlemen ; good night.
More torches here ! [*Guests all exeunt.*] Come on then,
  let 's to bed. [*L. U. E.*
Ah, sirrah, by my fay, it waxes late
I 'll to my rest.

> [*Exit* LADY CAPULET, OLD CAPULET *and* CAPULET,
> *L. 1 E. Lower lights.* JULIET *and* NURSE C., *re-*
> *enter* MERCUTIO *and* BENVOLIO. ROMEO *down L. H.*

JULIET.

Come hither, Nurse. What is yond gentleman ?
> [*Exit* BENVOLIO *L. U. E.*

NURSE.

[*R. of her.*] The son and heir of old Tiberio.

JULIET.

[*R. C.*] What 's he that now is going out of door ?
> [*Exit* MERCUTIO *L. U. E.*

NURSE.

Marry, that, I think, be young Petruchio.

JULIET.

What 's he that fellow there, that would not dance ?
> [*Exit* ROMEO *L. U. E.*

NURSE.

I know not.

JULIET.

[*C.*] Go ask his name.
> [NURSE *crosses in front.* *Exit L. U. E.*
> If he be married,

My grave is like to be my wedding bed.

36

NURSE.

> [*Re-enters and down L. C.*

[*Returns L. of* JULIET.] His name is Romeo, and a Montague,
The only son of your great enemy.

JULIET.

[*R. C.*] My only love sprung from my only hate !
Too early seen unknown, and known too late !
Prodigious birth of love it is to me
That I must love a loathed enemy.

NURSE.

[*C. L.*] What 's this ? What 's this ?

JULIET.

> A rhyme I learn'd even now

Of one I danc'd withal.

> [LADY CAPULET *calls* JULIET *within L.*

NURSE.

> Anon, anon !

Come let 's away ; the strangers all are gone.

> [JULIET *and* NURSE *C.* JULIET *up to stairs.* NURSE *stands C.*

SCENE IV.—*Moonlight.* CAPULET's *Orchard* (*Same as Balcony Scene*). *Late Sunday night, or early Monday morning. Enter* ROMEO *R. U. E. to Gateway C.*

BENVOLIO.

[*Outside.*] Romeo! Romeo!

ROMEO.

[*At Gateway R. C.*] Can I go forward when my heart is here ?

Turn back, dull earth, and find thy centre out. [*He climbs the wall, and leaps down within it L. C.*]

BENVOLIO.

[*Calls outside R. U. E.*] Romeo! my cousin Romeo!
[*Entering R. U. E. at gateway.*
Romeo!

MERCUTIO.

[*Entering R. U. E.*] He is wise;
And, on my life, hath stol 'n him home to bed.

BENVOLIO.

He ran this way, and leap'd this orchard wall;
Call, good Mercutio.

MERCUTIO.

Nay, I 'll conjure too.—
Romeo! humours! madman! passion! lover!
Appear thou in the likeness of a sigh!
Speak but one rhyme, and I am satisfied;
Cry but " Ay me!" pronounce but "love" and "dove;"
Speak to my gossip Venus one fair word,
One nickname for her purblind son and heir!
He heareth not, he stirreth not, he moveth not;
The ape is dead, and I must conjure him.
I conjure thee by Rosaline's bright eyes,
By her high forehead and her scarlet lip,
That in thy likeness thou appear to us!

BENVOLIO.

An if he hear thee, thou wilt anger him.

ROMEO *and* JULIET

MERCUTIO.

This cannot anger him; my invocation
Is fair and honest and in his mistress' name
I conjure only but to raise up him.

BENVOLIO.

Come, he hath hid himself among these trees,
To be consorted with the humorous night;
Blind is his love and best befits the dark.

MERCUTIO.

Romeo, good night—I 'll to my truckly-bed;
This field-bed is too cold for me to sleep.
Come, shall we go ?

BENVOLIO.

Go, then; for 'tis in vain
To seek him here that means not to be found.   Good night,
Romeo.   [*Exeunt R. U. E.*
                    [*Re-enter* ROMEO, *inside wall, L. C.*

ROMEO.

[*Speaking after them.*]   He jests at scars that never felt a
wound—
          [*Light appears through curtains above at window L. 2. E.*
But, soft! what light through yonder window breaks ?
It is the east and Juliet is the sun—
Arise, fair sun, and kill the envious moon,
Who is already sick and pale with grief,
That thou her maid art far more fair than she.

                              [JULIET *enters on balcony L.*
It *is* my lady, O, it is my love!
O, that she knew she were!—

She speaks, yet she says nothing ; what of that ?
Her eye discourses ; I will answer it.
I am too bold, 'tis not to me she speaks.
Two of the fairest stars in all the heaven,
Having some business, do entreat her eyes
To twinkle in their spheres till they return.
What if her eyes were there, they in her head ?
The brightness of her cheek would shame those stars,
As daylight doth a lamp ; her eyes in heaven
Would through the airy region stream so bright
That birds would sing and think it were not night.
See, how she leans her cheek upon her hand !
O, that I were a glove upon that hand,
That I might touch that cheek !

JULIET.
Ay me !

ROMEO.
She speaks.—
O, speak again, bright angel ! for thou art
As glorious to this night, being o'er my head,
As is a winged messenger of heaven
Unto the white-upturned wondering eyes
Of mortals that fall back to gaze on him,
When he bestrides the lazy-pacing clouds
And sails upon the bosom of the air.

JULIET.
O Romeo, Romeo ! wherefore art thou Romeo ?
Deny thy father and refuse thy name ;
Or, if you wilt not, be but sworn my love,
And I 'll no longer be a Capulet.

ROMEO *and* JULIET

ROMEO.

[*Aside.*]   Shall I hear more, or shall I speak at this ?

JULIET.

'Tis but thy name that is my enemy ;
Thou art thyself, though not a Montague.
What 's in a name ? that which we call a rose
By any other name would smell as sweet ;
So Romeo would, were he not Romeo call'd,
Retain that dear perfection which he owes
Without that title.—Romeo, doff thy name,
And for that name, which is no part of thee,
Take all myself.

ROMEO.

[*Advancing C.*]   I take thee at thy word.

JULIET.

What man art thou that thus bescreen'd in night
So stumblest on my counsel ?

ROMEO.

By a name
I know not how to tell thee who I am.
My name, dear saint, is hateful to myself,
Because it is an enemy to thee.

JULIET.

My ears have yet not drunk a hundred words
Of that tongue's uttering, yet I know the sound.—
Art thou not Romeo, and a Montague ?

ROMEO.

Neither, fair maid, if either thee dislike.

ROMEO *and* JULIET

JULIET.

How cam'st thou hither, tell me, and wherefore?
The orchard walls are high and hard to climb,
And the place death, considering who thou art,
If any of my kinsmen find thee here.

ROMEO.

With love's light wings did I o'er-perch these walls,
For stony limits cannot hold love out;
And what love can do, that dares love attempt,
Therefore thy kinsmen are no let to me.

JULIET.

If they do see thee, they will murther thee.

ROMEO.

Alack, there lies more peril in thine eye
Than twenty of their swords; look thou but sweet,
And I am proof against their enmity.

JULIET.

I would not for the world they saw thee here.

ROMEO.

I have night's cloak to hide me from their eyes;
And but thou love me, let them find me here;
My life were better ended by their hate,
Than death prorogued, wanting of thy love.

JULIET.

By whose direction founds't thou out this place?

ROMEO *and* JULIET

ROMEO.

By love, that first did prompt me to inquire ;
He lent me counsel, and I lent him eyes.
I am no pilot ; yet, wert thou as far
As that vast shore wash'd with the farthest sea,
I would adventure for such merchandise.

JULIET.

Thou know'st the mask of night is on my face,
Else would a maiden blush bepaint my cheek
For that which thou hast heard me speak to-night.
Fain would I dwell on form, fain, fain deny
What I have spoke ; but farewell compliment !
Dost thou love me ?   I know thou wilt say ay,
And I will take thy word ; yet, if thou swear'st
Thou mayst prove false ; at lovers' perjuries,
They say, Jove laughs.   O gentle Romeo,
If thou dost love, pronounce it faithfully :
Or if thou think'st I am too quickly won,
I 'll frown and be perverse and say thee nay,
So thou wilt woo ; (*Action for* ROMEO.) but else, not for the world.
In truth, fair Montague, I am too fond,
And therefore thou mayst think my 'haviour light ;
But trust me, gentleman, I 'll prove more true
Than those that have more cunning to be strange.
I should have been more strange, I must confess,
But that thou overheard'st, ere I was ware,
My true love's passion ; therefore pardon me,
And not impute this yielding to light love,
Which the dark night hath so discovered.

ROMEO *and* JULIET

ROMEO.

Lady, by yonder blessed moon I swear—

JULIET.

O, swear not by the moon, th' inconstant moon,
That monthly changes in her circled orb,
Lest that thy love prove likewise variable.

ROMEO.

What shall I swear by ?

JULIET.

     Do not swear at all ;
Or, if thou wilt, swear by thy gracious self,
Which is the god of my idolatry,
And I 'll believe thee.

ROMEO.

    If my heart's dear love—

JULIET.

Well, do not swear. Although I joy in thee,
I have no joy of this contract to-night ;
It is too rash, too unadvis'd, too sudden,
Too like the lightning, which doth cease to be
Ere one can say ' It lightens.' Sweet, good night !
This bud of love, by summer's ripening breath,
May prove a beauteous flower when next we meet.
Good night, good night ! as sweet repose and rest
Come to thy heart as that within my breast !

ROMEO.

O, wilt thou leave me so unsatisfied ?

ROMEO *and* JULIET

JULIET.

What satisfaction canst thou have to-night?

ROMEO.

The exchange of thy love's faithful vow for mine.

JULIET.

I gave thee mine before thou didst request it;
And yet I would it were to give again.

ROMEO.

Wouldst thou withdraw it? for what purpose, love?

JULIET.

But to be frank, and give it thee again,
And yet I wish but for the thing I have:
My bounty is as boundless as the sea,
My love as deep; the more I give to thee,
The more I have, for both are infinite.
I hear some noise within; dear love, adieu!

NURSE.

[*Within L. 2 E.*] Madam!

JULIET.

Anon, good nurse!—Sweet Montague, be true.
Stay but a little, I will come again.   [*Exit.*

ROMEO.

O blessed, blessed night! I am afeard,
Being in night, all this is but a dream,
Too flattering-sweet to be substantial.
                            [*Re-enter* JULIET, *above.*

JULIET.

Three words, dear Romeo, and good night indeed.
If that thy bent of love be honourable,
Thy purpose marriage, send me word to-morrow,
By one that I 'll procure to come to thee,
Where and what time thou wilt perform the rite ;
And all my fortunes at thy feet I 'll lay,
And follow thee, my lord, throughout the world.

NURSE.

[*Within.*]   Madam!

JULIET.

I come, anon.—But if thou mean'st not well,
I do beseech thee—

NURSE.

[*Within.*]   Madam!

JULIET.

By and by, I come.—
To cease thy suit, and leave me to my grief ;
To-morrow will I send.

ROMEO.

So thrive my soul—

JULIET.

A thousand times good night !   [*Exit.*

ROMEO.

A thousand times the worse, to want thy light.—
Love goes toward love, as schoolboys from their books,
But love from love, toward school with heavy looks.
                              [*Retiring slowly, L. U. E.*
        [*Re-enter* JULIET *above.*

ROMEO *and* JULIET

JULIET.

Hist! Romeo, hist!—O, for a falconer's voice,
To lure this tassel-gentle back again!—
Romeo!

ROMEO.

[*Up C.*]   It is my soul that calls upon my name;
How silver sweet sound lovers' tongues by night,
Like softest music to attending ears.   [*Forward L.C.*

JULIET.

Romeo !

ROMEO.

   My dear ?

JULIET.

       At what o'clock to-morrow
Shall I send to thee ?

ROMEO.

      At the hour of nine.

JULIET.

I will not fail ; 'tis twenty years till then.
I have forgot why I did call thee back.

ROMEO.

Let me stand here till thou remember it.

JULIET.

I shall forget, to have thee still stand there,
Remembering how I love thy company.

ROMEO.

And I 'll still stay, to have thee still forget,
Forgetting any other home but this.   [*Long pause.*

ROMEO *and* JULIET

JULIET.

'Tis almost morning; I would have thee gone :
And yet no farther than a wanton's bird,
Who lets it hop a little from her hand,
Like a poor prisoner in his twisted gyves,
And with a silk thread plucks it back again,
So loving-jealous of his liberty.

ROMEO.

I would I were thy bird.

JULIET.

Sweet, so would I : '
Yet I should kill thee with much cherishing.
Good night, good night!   Parting is such sweet sorrow,
That I shall say good night till it be morrow.   [*Exit, above.*

ROMEO.

Sleep dwell upon thine eyes, peace in thy breast !
Would I were sleep and peace, so sweet to rest !
                                   [*Kneels to pick up rose.*

END OF FIRST ACT.

48

ACT II

SCENE I.—FRIAR LAURENCE'S *Cell.*   *Monday morning, about four.*
FRIAR LAURENCE *discovered at desk, reading.—A basket
near him.*

FRIAR LAURENCE.

THE grey-eyed morn smiles on the frowning
            night,
    Chequering the eastern clouds with streaks of
            light;
    And flecked darkness like a drunkard reels
    From forth day's path and Titan's fiery
            wheels;
Now, ere the sun advance his burning eye,
The day to cheer and night's dank dew to dry,
I must up-fill this osier cage of ours
With baleful weeds and precious-juiced flowers.
O, mickle is the powerful grace that lies
In herbs, plants, stones and their true qualities;
For naught so vile that on the earth doth live,
But to the earth some special good doth give,
Nor aught so good, but, strain'd from that fair use,

49

Revolts from true birth, stumbling on abuse;
Virtue itself turns vice, being misapplied,
And vice sometime 's by action dignified.
Within the infant rind of this small flower
Poison hath residence, and medicine power;
For this, being smelt, with that part cheers each part,
Being tasted, slays all senses with the heart.
Two such opposed kings encamp them still
In man as well as herbs,—grace and rude will;
And where the worser is predominant,
Full soon the canker death eats up that plant.

> [*Enter* ROMEO, *through door in partition.*

ROMEO.

[*Kneeling.*] Good morrow, father.

FRIAR LAURENCE.

[*Turning to* ROMEO.] Benedicite!
What early tongue so sweet saluteth me?—
Young son, it argues a distemper'd head
So soon to bid good morrow to thy bed:
Care keeps his watch in every old man's eye,
And where care lodges, sleep will never lie;
But where unbruised youth with unstuff'd brain [ROMEO *rises.*
Doth couch his limbs, there golden sleep doth reign.
Therefore thy earliness doth me assure
Thou art up-rous'd by some distemperature;
Or, if not so, then here I hit it right,
Our Romeo hath not been in bed to-night.

ROMEO.

The last is true; the sweeter rest was mine.

ROMEO *and* JULIET

FRIAR LAURENCE.

God pardon sin ! Wast thou with Rosaline ?

ROMEO.

With Rosaline, my ghostly father ? No ;
I have forgot that name, and that name's woe.

FRIAR LAURENCE.

That 's my good son ; but where hast thou been, then ?

ROMEO.

I 'll tell thee ere thou ask it me again.
I have been feasting with mine enemy ;
Where on a sudden one hath wounded me,
That 's by me wounded ; both our remedies
Within thy help and holy physic lies.

FRIAR LAURENCE.

Be plain, good son, and homely in thy drift ;
Riddling confession finds but riddling shrift.

ROMEO.

Then plainly know, my heart's dear love is set
On the fair daughter of rich Capulet ;
As mine on hers, so hers is set on mine ;
And all combin'd, save what thou must combine
By holy marriage. When and where and how
We met, we woo'd and made exchange of vow,
I 'll tell thee as we pass ; but this I pray,
That thou consent to marry us to-day.

ROMEO *and* JULIET

FRIAR LAURENCE.

Holy Saint Francis, what a change is here !
Is Rosaline, that thou didst love so dear,
So soon forsaken ?   Young men's love then lies
Not truly in their hearts, but in their eyes.

ROMEO.

Thou chid'st me oft for loving Rosaline.

FRIAR LAURENCE.

For doting, not for loving, pupil mine.

ROMEO.

I pray thee, chide not ; she whom I love now
Doth grace for grace and love for love allow ;
The other did not so.

FRIAR LAURENCE.

     O, she knew well,
Thy love did read by rote and could not spell.
But come, young waverer, come, go with me ;
In one respect I 'll thy assistant be ;
For this alliance may so happy prove,
To turn your households' rancour to pure love.

ROMEO.

O, let us hence !   I stand on sudden haste.   [*Exit to other room.*

FRIAR LAURENCE.

Wisely and slow ; they stumble that run fast.   [*Exeunt.*

ROMEO *and* JULIET

SCENE II. *A Street. Monday Morning about 8.30.*
[*Enter* BENVOLIO *and* MERCUTIO, *R. arcb R. U. E.*

MERCUTIO.

Where the devil should this Romeo be?
Came he not home to night?

BENVOLIO.

Not to his father's; I spoke with his man.

MERCUTIO.

Why, that same pale hard-hearted wench, that Rosaline,
Torments him so that he will sure ran mad.

BENVOLIO.

Tybalt, the kinsman of old Capulet,
Hath sent a letter to his father's house.

MERCUTIO.

A challenge, on my life.

BENVOLIO.

Romeo will answer it.

MERCUTIO.

Any man that can write may answer a letter.

BENVOLIO.

Nay, he will answer the letter's master, how he dares, being
dared.

MERCUTIO.

Alas, poor Romeo he is already dead! stabbed with a white
wench's black eye; shot through the ear with a love-song; the

very pin of his heart cleft with the blind bow-boy's butt-shaft : and is he a man to encounter Tybalt ?

BENVOLIO.

Why, what is Tybalt ?

MERCUTIO.

More than prince of cats, I can tell you. O, he's the courage-ous captain of compliments. He fights as you sing prick-song, keeps time, distance and proportion ; rests me his minim rest, one, two, and the third in your bosom : the very butcher of a silk button, a duellist, a duellist ; a gentleman of the very first house, of the first and second cause. Ah, the immortal passado ! the punto reverso ! the hai !

BENVOLIO.

The what ?

MERCUTIO.

The plague of such antic, lisping, affecting fantasticoes, these new tuners of accents ! 'By Jesu, a very good blade ! a very tall man ! A very fine wench.' Why, is not this a lamentable thing, grand-sire, that we should be thus afflicted with these strange flies, these fashion-mongers, these *pardonnez-moi's ?* O, their *bons,* their *bons !*

BENVOLIO.

[*Looking off R. U. E.*] Here comes Romeo, here comes Romeo.

MERCUTIO.

Without his roe, like a dried herring : O flesh, flesh, how art thou fishified ! Now is he for the numbers that Petrarch flowed in : Laura to his lady was but a kitchen-wench ; marry, she had a better love to be-rhyme her ; Dido a dowdy ; Cleopatra a

gipsy ; Helen and Hero, hildings and harlots ;   Thisbe a grey
eye or so, but not to the purpose.—

[*Enter* ROMEO *R. U. E. through arch.*

Signior Romeo, *bon jour !* there 's a French salutation for you.
You gave us the counterfeit fairly last night.

ROMEO.

Good morrow to you both.   What counterfeit did I give you ?

MERCUTIO.

The slip, sir, the slip.   Can you not conceive ?

ROMEO.

Pardon, good Mercutio, my business was great ; and in such a
case as mine a man may strain courtesy.

MERCUTIO.

A sail, a sail !   [*Looking off R.*

BENVOLIO.

Two, two ; a shirt and a smock.

[*Enter* PETER *and* NURSE *R. 2 E.*

NURSE.

Peter !

PETER.

Anon !

NURSE.

My fan, Peter.   [PETER *gives fan to* NURSE.

MERCUTIO.

Good Peter, to hide her face, for her fan 's the fairer of the two.

NURSE.

God ye good morrow, gentlemen.

MERCUTIO.

[*Crossing to* NURSE.]   God ye good den, fair gentlewoman.

NURSE.

Gentlemen, can any one of you tell me where I may find the young Romeo ?

[MERCUTIO *and* BENVOLIO *laugh.*

ROMEO.

I am the youngest of that name, for fault of a worse.

NURSE.

You say well.   [PETER *sits on steps of church.*]   If you be he, sir, I desire some confidence with you.

BENVOLIO.

She will indite him to some supper.

MERCUTIO.

So ho!   [*Catches* ROMEO's *eye.*]   Romeo, will you come to your father's ?   We 'll to dinner, thither.

ROMEO.

I will follow you.

MERCUTIO.

Farewell, ancient lady ; farewell,   [*Singing.*
' Lady, lady, lady.'

[*Exeunt* MERCUTIO *and* BENVOLIO, R. 2 E.

NURSE.

Marry, farewell!—I pray you, sir, what saucy merchant was this, that was so full of his ropery ?

ROMEO *and* JULIET

ROMEO.

A gentleman, nurse, that loves to hear himself talk, and will speak more in a minute than he will stand to in a month.

NURSE.

Scurvy knave! I am none of his flirt-gills; I am none of his skains-mates. [*Sees* PETER; *goes up to him and hits him with fan.*] And thou must stand by, too, and suffer every knave to use me at his pleasure?

PETER.

I saw no man use you at his pleasure; if I had, my weapon should quickly have been out, I warrant you. I dare draw as soon as another man, if I see occasion in a good quarrel, and the law on my side.

NURSE.

Scurvy knave!—Pray you, sir, a word: and as I told you, my young lady bade me inquire you out; what she bade me say, I will keep to myself: but first let me tell ye, if ye should lead her into a fool's paradise, as they say, it were a very gross kind of behavior, as they say: for the gentlewoman is young, and therefore if you should deal double with her, truly it were an ill thing to be offered to any gentlewoman, and very weak dealing.

ROMEO.

Nurse, commend me to thy lady and mistress. I protest unto thee—

NURSE.

Good heart, and, i' faith, I will tell her as much. Lord, Lord, she will be a joyful woman.   [*Going toward R.*

ROMEO.

What wilt thou tell her, nurse? Thou dost not mark me.

NURSE.

I will tell her, sir, that you do protest; which, as I take it, is a gentlemanlike offer.

ROMEO.

     Bid her devise
Some means to come to shrift this afternoon;
And there she shall at Friar Laurence' cell
Be shriv'd and married. Here is for thy pains.

NURSE.

No, truly, sir; not a penny.

ROMEO.

Go to; I say you shall.

NURSE.

This afternoon, sir? Well, she shall be there.

ROMEO.

And stay, good nurse; behind the abbey wall
Within this hour my man shall be with thee,
And bring thee cords made like a tackled stair;
Which to the high top-gallant of my joy
Must be my convoy in the secret night.
Farewell; be trusty, and I 'll quit thy pains;
Farewell; commend me to thy mistress.

NURSE.

Now God in heaven bless thee!

ROMEO.

Commend me to thy lady.

NURSE.

Ay, a thousand times— [*Exit* ROMEO, *L. 2 E.*] Peter !
[*Pokes him with cane.*

PETER.

Anon !

NURSE.

[*Giving fan to him.*] Before and apace.

[*Exeunt, R. 2 E.*

SCENE III.—CAPULET's *Garden. Monday morning.* JULIET *discovered, C., looking off L. 1 E.*

JULIET.

The clock struck nine when I did send the nurse ;
In half an hour she promised to return.
Perchance she cannot meet him ; that 's not so.
O, she is lame ! love's heralds should be thoughts,
Which ten times faster glide than the sun's beams
Driving back shadows over louring hills ;
Therefore do nimble-pinion'd doves draw love,
And therefore hath the wind-swift Cupid wings.
Now is the sun upon the highmost hill
Of this day's journey, and from nine till twelve
Is three long hours, yet she is not come.
Had she affections and warm, youthful blood,
She would be as swift in motion as a ball ;
My words would bandy her to my sweet love,
And his to me :
But old folks, many feign as they were dead ;
Unwieldy, slow, heavy and pale as lead. [*About to sit R. C.*
        [*Enter* NURSE *and* PETER *L. 1 E.*
O God, she comes !—O honey nurse, what news ?
Hast thou met with him ? Send thy man away.

ROMEO *and* JULIET

NURSE.

Peter, stay at the gate.   [*Exit* PETER, *L. 1 E.*

JULIET.

Now, good sweet nurse,—O Lord, why look'st thou sad?

NURSE.

I am a-weary; give me leave a while.
Fie, how my bones ache! What a jaunt have I had!

[*Sits R. C.*

JULIET.

I would thou hadst my bones, and I thy news.
Nay, come, I pray thee, speak; good, good nurse, speak.

NURSE.

Jesu, what haste! Can you not stay awhile?
Do you not see that I am out of breath?

JULIET.

How art thou out of breath, when thou hast breath
To say to me that thou art out of breath?
The excuse that thou dost make in this delay
Is longer than the tale thou dost excuse.
Is thy news good or bad? Answer to that;
Say either, and I'll stay the circumstance:
Let me be satisfied, is 't good or bad?

NURSE.

Well, you have made a simple choice; you know not how to
choose a man. Romeo! No, not he; though his face be better
than any man's, yet his leg excels all men's; and as for a hand,
and a foot, and a body, though they be not to be talked on, yet
they are past compare; he is not the flower of courtesy, but I'll

60

warrant him as gentle as a lamb. Go thy ways, wench; serve
God.—What, have you dined at home?

JULIET.

No, no; but all this did I know before.
What says he of our marriage? what of that?

NURSE.

Lord, how my head aches! What a head have I!
It beats as it would fall in twenty pieces.
My back o' t' other side,—O, my back, my back!
Beshrew your heart for sending me about,
To catch my death with jaunting up and down!

JULIET.

I' faith, I am sorry that thou art not well.
Sweet, sweet, sweet nurse, tell me, what says my love?

NURSE.

Your love says, like an honest gentleman, and a courteous, and
a kind, and a handsome, and, I warrant, a virtuous,—Where is
your mother?

JULIET.

Where is my mother! Why, she is within;
Where should she be? How oddly thou repliest!
' Your love says, like an honest gentleman,
Where is your mother?'

NURSE.

O God's lady dear!
Are you so hot? Marry, come up, I trow;
Is this the poultice for my aching bones?
Henceforward do your messages yourself.

[NURSE *rises and goes up C., as if going.*

ROMEO *and* JULIET

JULIET.

Here 's such a coil!—come, what says Romeo ? [NURSE *returns.*

NURSE.

Have you got leave to go to shrift to-day ?

JULIET.

I have.

NURSE.

Then hie you hence to Friar Laurence' cell ;
There stays a husband to make you a wife.
Now comes the wanton blood up in your cheeks,
They 'll be in scarlet straight at any news.
Go; I 'll to dinner; hie you to the cell.

[JULIET *crosses to L.*

JULIET.

Hie to high fortune !—Honest nurse, [*Kisses her.*] farewell.

[NURSE *goes up C. Exit* JULIET *L. 1 E.*

END OF SECOND ACT.

62

ACT III

Scene I. Friar Laurence's *cell.* *Monaay—about noon.* Enter Romeo *and* Friar Laurence *L. C.*

Friar Laurence.

SO SMILE the heavens upon this holy act
That after-hours with sorrow chide us not!

Romeo.

Amen, amen! but come what sorrow can,
It cannot countervail the exchange of joy
That one short minute gives me in her sight.
Do thou but close our hands with holy words,
Then love-devouring death do what he dare,
It is enough I may but call her mine.

Friar Laurence.

These violent delights have violent ends,
And in their triumphs die, like fire and powder,
Which as they kiss consume:

63

Therefore, love moderately ; long love doth so ;
Too swift arrives as tardy as too slow.

[*Enter* JULIET *C. L.*

Here comes the lady. [FRIAR *goes to her and leads her into cell.*
· O, so light a foot
Will ne'er wear out the everlasting flint !

JULIET.

Good even to my ghostly confessor.

FRIAR LAURENCE.

Romeo shall thank thee, daughter, for us both.

JULIET.

As much to him, else is his thanks too much.

ROMEO.

Ah, Juliet, if the measure of thy joy
Be heap'd like mine, and that thy skill be more
To blazon it, then sweeten with thy breath
This neighbor air, and let rich music's tongue
Unfold the imagin'd happiness that both
Receive in either by this dear encounter.

JULIET.

Conceit, more rich in matter than in words,
Brags of his substance, not of ornament.
They are but beggars that can count their worth ;
But my true love is grown to such excess
I cannot sum up half my sum of wealth.

FRIAR LAURENCE.

[*Down R. H.*] Come, come with me, and we will make short work ;

For, by your leaves, you shall not stay alone [*Opens door R. 1 E.*

Till holy church incorporate two in one.

                        [*Exeunt R. 1 E.*

SCENE II.—*A Public Place.*   *Monday; the early afternoon.*   *Enter* MERCUTIO, BENVOLIO, *Page, Lords and Servants,* *L. U. E.*

BENVOLIO.

I pray thee, good Mercutio, let 's retire :

The day is hot, the Capulets abroad,

And if we meet we shall not 'scape a brawl ;

For now, these hot days, is the mad blood stirring.

MERCUTIO.

Thou art like one of those fellows that when he enters the confines of a tavern claps me his sword upon the table, and says ' God send me no need of thee ! ' and by the operation of the second cup draws him on the drawer when indeed there is no need.

BENVOLIO.

[*Hotly.*]   Am I like such a fellow ?

MERCUTIO.

Come, come, thou art as hot a Jack in thy mood as any in Italy, and as soon moved to be moody, and as soon moody to be moved.

BENVOLIO.

And what to ?

MERCUTIO.

Nay, an there were two such, we should have none shortly, for one would kill the other. Thou! Why, thou wilt quarrel with a man that hath a hair more, or a hair less in his beard than thou hast. Thou wilt quarrel with a man for cracking nuts, having no other reason but because thou hast hazel eyes. Thou hast quarrelled with a man for coughing in the street, because he hath wakened thy dog that hath lain asleep in the sun. Didst thou not fall out with a tailor for wearing his new doublet before Easter? with another, for trying his new shoes with old riband? and yet thou wilt tutor me from quarrelling!

BENVOLIO.

An I were so apt to quarrel as thou art, any man should buy the fee-simple of my life for an hour and a quarter.

MERCUTIO.

The fee-simple! O simple!

BENVOLIO.

[*Looking off R.*] By my head, here come the Capulets.

MERCUTIO.

By my heel, I care not.

[*Enter* TYBALT, *three Lords, three Servants and others,* R. U. E.

TYBALT.

Follow me close, for I will speak to them.—
Gentlemen, good den; a word with one of you.

MERCUTIO.

And but one word with one of us? Couple it with something; make it a word and a blow.

TYBALT.

You shall find me apt enough to that, sir, an you will give me occasion.

MERCUTIO.

Could you not take some occasion without giving?

TYBALT.

Mercutio, thou consort'st with Romeo,—

MERCUTIO.

Consort! What, dost thou make us minstrels? an thou make minstrels of us, look to hear nothing but discords: here's my fiddlestick; here's that shall make you dance. 'Zounds, consort!

BENVOLIO.

[*Between them.*] We talk here in the public haunt of men,
Either withdraw unto some private place,
Or reason coldly of your grievances,
Or else depart; here all eyes gaze on us.

MERCUTIO.

Men's eyes were made to look, and let them gaze;
I will not budge for no man's pleasure, I.

TYBALT.

Well, peace be with you, sir; here comes my man.
[*Enter* ROMEO, *R. 1 E.*

MERCUTIO.

But I'll be hanged, sir, if he wear your livery.
[*Goes up to* BENVOLIO.

67

ROMEO *and* JULIET

TYBALT.

Romeo, the hate I bear thee can afford
No better term than this,—thou art a villain.

ROMEO.

Tybalt, the reason that I have to love thee
Doth much excuse the appertaining rage
To such a greeting.   Villain am I none ;
Therefore, farewell ; I see thou know'st me not.

        [Crosses and goes up to MERCUTIO *and* BENVOLIO.

TYBALT.

Boy, this shall not excuse the injuries
That thou hast done me ; therefore, turn and draw.

ROMEO.

I do protest, I never injur'd thee,
But love thee better than thou canst devise,
Till thou shalt know the reason of my love ;
And so, good Capulet,—which name I tender
As dearly as mine own,—be satisfied.   *[Exit L. 2 E.*

MERCUTIO.

O calm, dishonorable, vile submission !

  *[*TYBALT *and his partisans, laughing derisively, are moving away*
R. C.

   Alla stoccata carries it away.   *[He draws.*
   Tybalt, you rat-catcher, will you walk ?

TYBALT.

What would thou have with me ?   *[Returning down R. C.*

ROMEO *and* JULIET

MERCUTIO.

Good king of cats, nothing but one of your nine lives, that I mean to make bold withal. Will you pluck your sword out of its pilcher by the ears ? Make haste, lest mine be about your ears ere it be out.

TYBALT.

[*Drawing.*] I am for you.

ROMEO.

[*Re-entering L. 2 E.*] Gentle Mercutio, put thy rapier up.

MERCUTIO.

Come, sir, your passado. [*They fight.*

ROMEO.

Draw, Benvolio ; beat down their weapons.
Gentlemen, for shame, forbear this outrage.
Tybalt, Mercutio, the prince expressly hath
Forbid this bandying in Verona streets.
Hold, Tybalt ! Good Mercutio ! [TYBALT *stabs* MERCUTIO.
  [*Exeunt* TYBALT *and his partisans, R. U. E.*

MERCUTIO.

[ROMEO *and* BENVOLIO *catch him.*] I am hurt.
A plague o' both your houses ! I am sped.
Is he gone, and hath nothing ?

BENVOLIO.

What, art thou hurt ?

MERCUTIO.

Ay, ay, a scratch, a scratch ; marry, 'tis enough.—
Where is my page ? Go, villain, fetch a surgeon.
  [*Exit Page R. U. E.*

69

ROMEO *and* JULIET

ROMEO.

Courage, man ; the hurt cannot be much.

MERCUTIO.

No, 'tis not so deep as a well, nor so wide as a church door ;
but 'tis enough, 'twill serve : I am peppered, I warrant, for this
world.—A plague o' both your houses !—'Zounds, a dog, a rat,
a mouse, a cat, to scratch a man to death! a braggart, a rogue, a
villain, that fights by the book of arithmetic!—Why the devil
came you between us ? I was hurt under your arm.

ROMEO.

I thought all for the best.

MERCUTIO.

Help me into some house, Benvolio,
Or I shall faint.—A plague of both your houses!
They have made worms' meat of me. I have it,
And soundly too ; ask for me to-morrow, and you shall find me
a grave man : Your houses !
    [*Exeunt* MERCUTIO *and* BENVOLIO, *L. 2 E.*

ROMEO.

This gentleman, the prince's near ally,
My very friend, hath got his mortal hurt
In my behalf ; my reputation stain'd
With Tybalt's slander,—Tybalt, that an hour
Hath been my cousin !—O sweet Juliet,
Thy beauty hath made me effeminate,
And in my temper soften'd valour's steel !
    [*Re-enter* BENVOLIO.

70

ROMEO *and* JULIET

BENVOLIO.

O Romeo, Romeo, brave Mercutio's dead!

[*Looking off R. C.*

Here comes the furious Tybalt back again.

[*Re-enter* TYBALT.

ROMEO.

Alive, in triumph! and Mercutio slain!

[*Picks up* MERCUTIO's *sword.*

Now, Tybalt, take the 'villain' back again
That late thou gavest me, for Mercutio's soul
Is but a little way above our heads.
Staying for thine to keep him company;
Either thou, or I, or both, must go with him.

TYBALT.

Thou, wretched boy, that didst consort him here,
Shalt with him hence.

ROMEO.

This shall determine that.

[*They fight.* TYBALT *falls. Bell. Murmurs within.*

BENVOLIO.

Romeo, away, be gone!
The citizens are up, and Tybalt slain,
Stand not amaz'd; the prince will doom thee death,
If thou art taken. Hence, be gone, away!

ROMEO.

[*Up C.*] O, I am fortune's fool!

[*Exit* ROMEO *and* BENVOLIO, *L. U. E. Enter officer,
guards and servants of Prince, citizens, etc.*

ROMEO *and* JULIET

SCENE III.—FRIAR LAURENCE's *Cell.   Monday afternoon.*   ROMEO
discovered.   Enter FRIAR LAURENCE, *who locks iron gates.*

FRIAR LAURENCE.
Romeo !

ROMEO.
[*In chair, R. C.*]   Father, what news ?   What is the prince's
doom ?
What sorrow craves acquaintance at my hand,
That I yet know not ?

FRIAR LAURENCE.
Too familiar
Is my dear son with such sour company ;
I bring thee tidings of the prince's doom.

ROMEO.
What less than doomsday is the prince's doom ?

FRIAR LAURENCE.
A gentler judgment vanished from his lips,
Not body's death, but body's banishment.

ROMEO.
[*Rises.*]   Ha, banishment ! be merciful, say death ;
For exile hath more terror in his look,
Much more than death ; do not say banishment.

FRIAR LAURENCE.
Hence from Verona art thou banished.
Be patient, for the world is broad and wide.

ROMEO *and* JULIET

ROMEO.

There is no world without Verona walls,
But purgatory, torture, hell itself.
Hence banished is banish'd from the world,
And world's exile is death : then banished
Is death mis-term'd ; calling death banishment
Thou cutt'st my head off with a golden axe,
And smil'st upon the stroke that murthers me.

FRIAR LAURENCE.

O deadly sin !   O rude unthankfulness !
Thy fault our law calls death ; but the kind prince,
Taking thy part, hath rush'd aside the law,
And turn'd that black word death to banishment.

ROMEO.

'Tis torture and not mercy !   Heaven is here
Where Juliet lives ; and every cat and dog
And little mouse, every unworthy thing,
Live here in heaven and may look on her,
But Romeo may not.
Hadst thou no poison mix'd, no sharp-ground knife,
No sudden mean of death, though ne'er so mean,
But 'banished' to kill me ?—Banished !
O friar, the damned use that word in hell :
Howling attends it : how hast thou the heart,
Being a divine, a ghostly confessor,
A sin-absolver, and my friend profess'd,
To mangle me with that word 'banished ?'

FRIAR LAURENCE.

Thou fond mad man, hear me but speak a word.

ROMEO.

O, thou wilt speak again of banishment.   [*In chair R. C.*

FRIAR LAURENCE.

I 'll give thee armor to keep off that word ;
Adversity's sweet milk, philosophy.
To comfort thee, though thou art banished.

ROMEO.

[*Rises.*]   Yet 'banished !'   Hang up philosophy !
Unless philosophy can make a Juliet,
Displant a town, reverse a prince's doom,
It helps not, it prevails not ; talk no more.

FRIAR LAURENCE.

Let me dispute with thee of thy estate.

ROMEO.

Thou canst not speak of that thou dost not feel.
Wert thou as young as I, Juliet thy love,
An hour but married, Tybalt murthered,
Doting like me and like me banished,
Then mightst thou speak, then mightst thou tear thy hair,
And fall upon the ground, as I do now,   [*Falls R. C.*
Taking the measure of an unmade grave.
      [*Knocking within.   Nurse at gate L. C.*

FRIAR LAURENCE.

Arise ; one knocks ; good Romeo, hide thyself.
                                    [*Knocking.*

Hark, how they knock !—Who 's there ?—Romeo, arise ;
Thou wilt be taken.—Stay awhile !—Stand up !

                                           [*Knock.*

                 By and by !—God's will.

What simpleness is this !—

                                       [*Knocking.*

                 I come, I come.

Who knocks so hard ?   Whence come you ?   What 's your
will ?

N u r s e.

[*Within.*]   Let me come in, and you shall know my errand ;
I come from Lady Juliet.

F r i a r   L a u r e n c e.

                 Welcome, then.

     [*Enter* Nurse.

N u r s e.

O holy friar, O, tell me, holy friar,
Where is my lady's lord, where 's Romeo ?

F r i a r   L a u r e n c e.

There on the ground, with his own tears made drunk.

N u r s e.

O, he is even in my mistress' case,
Just in her case !   Stand up, my lord !
For Juliet's sake, for her sake, rise and stand.

R o m e o.

Spak'st thou of Juliet ?   How is it with her ?

N u r s e.

O, she says nothing, sir, but weeps and weeps ;

And now falls on her bed ; and then starts up,
And Tybalt calls ; and then on Romeo cries,
And then down falls again.

ROMEO.

As if that name,
Shot from the deadly level of a gun,
Did murther her ;—O, tell me, friar, tell me,
In what vile part of this anatomy
Doth my name lodge ?   Tell me, that I may sack
The hateful mansion.

[*Drawing his dagger, on knees,* R. C.

FRIAR LAURENCE.

[*Seizing his hand.*]   Hold thy desperate hand !
Art thou a man ? thy form cries out thou art ;
Thy tears are womanish ; thy wild acts denote
The unreasonable fury of a beast ;
Thou hast amaz'd me ; by my holy order,
I thought thy disposition better temper'd.
Hast thou slain Tybalt ? wilt thou slay thyself ?
And slay thy lady too, that lives in thee,
By doing damned hate upon thyself ?
What, rouse thee, man ! thy Juliet is alive,
There art thou happy; Tybalt would kill thee,
But thou slew'st Tybalt ; there art thou happy too ;
The law that threaten'd death becomes thy friend
And turns it to exile ; there art thou happy.
A pack of blessings lights upon thy back,
Happiness courts thee in her best array ;
But, like a misbehaved and sullen wench,

Thou pout'st upon thy fortune and thy love;
Take heed, take heed, for such die miserable.
Go, get thee to thy love, as was decreed;
But look thou, stay not till the watch be set,
For then thou canst not pass to Mantua;
Where thou shalt live, till we can find a time
To blame your marriage, reconcile your friends,
Beg pardon of the prince, and call thee back
With twenty hundred thousand times more joy
Than thou went'st forth in lamentation. [ROMEO *rises.*
Go before, nurse; commend me to thy lady.
Romeo is coming.

NURSE.

O Lord, I could have stay'd here all the night
To hear good counsel; O what learning is!
My lord, I 'll tell my lady you will come.

ROMEO.

Do so, and bid my sweet prepare to chide.

NURSE.

Here, sir, a ring she bid me give you, sir;
Hie you, make haste, for it grows very late.

[*Exit.*

ROMEO.

How well my comfort is reviv'd by this!

FRIAR LAURENCE.

Go hence; good night; and here stands all you state:
Either be gone before the watch be set,
Or by the break of day disguis'd from hence.

ACT IV

Scene I. Juliet's *chamber. Tuesday—early morning.* Romeo *and* Juliet *discovered, seated on couch,* C.

JULIET.

ILT thou be gone? It is not yet near day:
It was the nightingale, and not the lark,
That pierced the fearful hollow of thine ear;
Nightly she sings on yond pomegranate-tree.
Believe me, love, it was the nightingale.

ROMEO.

It was the lark, the herald of the morn,
No nightingale; look, love, what envious streaks
Do lace the severing clouds in yonder east.
Night's candles are burnt out, and jocund day
Stands tiptoe on the misty mountain tops.
I must be gone and live, or stay and die.

ROMEO *and* JULIET

JULIET.

Yon light is not day-light, I know it, I :
It is some meteor that the sun exhales,
To be to thee this night a torch-bearer,
And light thee on thy way to Mantua.
Therefore stay yet ; thou need'st not to be gone.

ROMEO.

Let me be ta'en, let me be put to death,
I am content ; so thou wilt have it so.
I 'll say yon gray is not the morning's eye,
'Tis but the pale reflex of Cynthia's brow ;
Nor that is not the lark whose notes do beat
The vaulty heavens so high above our heads.
I have more care to stay than will to go ;
Come, death, and welcome ! Juliet wills it so.
How is 't, my soul ?   Let 's talk ; it is not day.

JULIET.

    [*Rises and crosses to window, R. 1 E., opening on balcony.*
It is, it is, hie hence, be gone, away !
It is the lark that sings so out of tune, [*Returns to end of couch.*
Straining harsh discords and unpleasant sharps.
Some say the lark makes sweet division ;
This doth not so, for she divideth us.
Some say the lark and loathed toad changed eyes ;
O, now I would they had changed voices too !
Since arm from arm that voice doth us affray,
Hunting thee hence with hunts-up to the day,
O, now be gone ; more light and light it grows. [*Moving to R.*

80

ROMEO *and* JULIET

ROMEO.

More light and light : more dark and dark our woes!   [*Rises.*
　　[*Enter* NURSE *L. U. E.*

NURSE.

Madam !

JULIET.

[*Starts.*]   Nurse ?

NURSE.

Your lady mother is coming to your chamber,
The day is broke ; be wary, look about.

JULIET.

[*Looks at* ROMEO, *goes to window, R., and opens it.*]   Then,
　　window, let day in, and let life out.

ROMEO.

Farewell, farewell ! One kiss, and I 'll descend. [*About to go.*

JULIET.

Art thou gone so ?　　　　　　　　　　　[ROMEO *returns.*
　　　　　My lord, my love, my friend!
I must hear from thee every day in the hour,
For in a minute there are many days.
O, by this count I shall be much in years
Ere I again behold my Romeo !

ROMEO.

Farewell !
I will omit no opportunity
That may convey my greetings, love, to thee.

JULIET.

O, think'st thou we shall ever meet again ?

ROMEO *and* JULIET

JULIET.

[*L. of table L. C.*]   Yet let me weep for such a feeling loss.

LADY CAPULET.

Well, girl, thou weep'st not so much for his death
As that the villian lives which slaughter'd him.

JULIET.

What villain, madam?

LADY CAPULET.

That same villain, Romeo.

JULIET.

Villain and he be many miles asunder.
God pardon him!   I do, with all my heart;
And yet no man like he doth grieve my heart.

LADY CAPULET.

That is because the traitor murderer lives.
But now I tell you joyful tidings, girl.

JULIET.

And joy comes well in such a needy time.
What are they, I beseech your ladyship?

LADY CAPULET.

Well, well, thou hast a careful father, child;
One who, to put thee from thy heaviness,
Hath sorted out a sudden day of joy
That thou expect'st not, nor I look'd not for
Early next Thursday morn,
The gallant, young and noble gentleman,

ROMEO *and* JULIET

The County Paris, at Saint Peter's Church,
Shall happily make thee there a joyful bride.

> [JULIET *crosses to window R.*

JULIET.

Now by Saint Peter's Church and Peter too
He shall not make me there a joyful bride.

> [LADY CAPULET *rises.*

I wonder at this haste ; that I must wed
Ere he that should be husband comes to woo.
I pray you tell my lord and father, Madam,
I will not marry yet.

LADY CAPULET.

Here comes your father ; [*Looking off L.*

> [*Enter* CAPULET *and* NURSE, *L.*

Tell him so yourself,
And see how he will take it at your hands.

CAPULET.

How now, a conduit, girl ? what ; still in tears ?
Evermore showering ?—How now, wife
Have you deliver'd to her our decree ?

LADY CAPULET.

Ay, sir ; but she will none, she gives you thanks.
I would the fool were married to her grave.

> [*Crosses to L. back of couch.* NURSE *moves to C. above her.*

CAPULET.

Soft ! take me with you, take me with you, wife.
How ! will she none ? doth she not give us thanks !

84

Is she not proud? doth she not count her blest,
Unworthy as she is, that we have wrought
So worthy a gentleman to be her bridegroom?

                    [LADY CAPULET *L. of table, sits.*

JULIET.

Not proud you have, but thankful that you have;
Proud can I never be of what I hate;
But thankful even for hate that is meant love.

CAPULET.

How now, how now, chop-logic! What is this?
'Proud' and 'I thank you' and 'I thank you not,'
And yet 'not proud;' mistress minion, you,
Thank me no thankings, nor proud me no prouds,
But fettle your fine joints 'gainst Thursday next,
To go with Paris to Saint Peter's Church,
Or I will drag thee on a hurdle thither.

JULIET.

Good father, I beseech you on my knees,
Hear me with patience but to speak a word.

CAPULET.

Hang thee, young baggage! disobedient wretch!
I tell thee what: get thee to church o' Thursday,
Or never after look me in the face.
Speak not, reply not, do not answer me;
My fingers itch. Wife, we scarce thought us blest
That God had lent us but this only child;
But now I see this one is one too much,
And that we have a curse in having her;
Out on her hilding! [*Crosses to R. and up C.*

I am too young ; I pray you pardon me ?'
But, an you will not wed, I 'll pardon you ;
Graze where you will, you shall not house with me :
Look to 't, think on 't, I do not use to jest,   [*Moves to L.*
An you be mine, I 'll give you to my friend ;
An you be not, hang, beg, starve, die in the streets,
For, by my soul, I 'll ne'er acknowledge thee.   [*Exit L. 1 E.*

JULIET.

[*C.*]   Is there no pity sitting in the clouds,
That sees into the bottom of my grief ?

     [LADY CAPULET *moves to L., as if to follow* CAPULET.
O, sweet my mother, cast me not away !
Delay this marriage for a month, a week ;
Or, if you do not, make the bridal bed
In that dim monument where Tybalt lies.

           [NURSE *comes slowly down R. C.*

LADY CAPULET.

Talk not to me, for I 'll not speak a word ;
Do as thou wilt, for I have done with thee.   [*Exit.*

JULIET.

[*Sinking down.*]   O God !   [NURSE *goes to her.*]   O nurse,
how shall this be prevented ?
Comfort me, counsel me.   [NURSE *helps her to couch.*
Alack, alack, that heaven should practice stratagems
Upon so soft a subject as myself !
What say'st thou ? hast thou not a word of joy ?
Some comfort, nurse.

NURSE.

Faith, here 't is.   Romeo
Is banish'd, and all the world to nothing
That he dares ne'er come back to challenge you;
Or, if he do, it needs must be by stealth.
Then, since the case so stands as now it doth,
I think it best you married with the County.
Oh, he 's a gallant gentleman.
Romeo 's a dish-clout to him; an eagle, madam,
Hath not so green, so quick, so fair an eye
As Paris hath.   Beshrew my very heart,
I think you are happy in this second match,
For it excels your first; or if it did not
Your first is dead, or 'twere as good he were.

JULIET.

[*Seated on couch.*]   Speakest thou from thy heart?

NURSE.

[*Standing R. of her.*]   And from my soul too;
Or else beshrew them both.

JULIET.

Amen !

NURSE.

What ?

JULIET.

Well, thou hast comforted me marvellous much,
        [NURSE *goes towards her.* JULIET *draws back; then
        goes to R. H.*
Go in, and tell my lady I am gone,

Having displeased my father, to Laurence's cell,
To make confession and to be absolved.

N U R S E.

Marry, I will ; and this is wisely done.   [*Exit L.*

J U L I E T.

[*R. C.*]   O most wicked fiend !
Is it more sin to wish me thus foresworn,
Or to dispraise my lord with that same tongue
Which she hath prais'd him with above compare
So many thousand times ? Go, counsellor ;
Thou and my bosom henceforth shall be twain
I 'll to the friar, to know his remedy :
          [*Goes up C. back of table ; takes up dagger.*
If all else fail, myself have power to die.   [*Exit L.*

SCENE II.—FRIAR LAURENCE'S *Cell. Tuesday morning.* FRIAR
          LAURENCE *and* PARIS *discovered.* FRIAR LAURENCE *seated
          R. C.;* PARIS *standing C.*

F R I A R   L A U R E N C E.

On Thursday, sir ? the time is very short.

P A R I S.

My father Capulet will have it so ;
And I am nothing slow to slack his haste.

F R I A R   L A U R E N C E.

You say you do not know the lady's mind.
Uneven is the course, I like it not.

.   **89**

ROMEO *and* JULIET

PARIS.

Immoderately she weeps for Tybalt's death,
And therefore have I little talk'd of love ;
For Venus smiles not in a house of tears.
Now, sir, her father counts it dangerous
That she doth give her sorrow so much sway,
And in his wisdom hastes our marriage,
To stop the inundation of her tears.
Now do you know the reason of this haste.

FRIAR LAURENCE.

[*Aside.*] I would I knew not why it should be slow'd.

    [*Enter* JULIET *through gate, L. C.* FRIAR LAURENCE
    sees her and rises.

PARIS.

[*Turns, on* FRIAR LAURENCE'S *action, and sees her.*] Happily
met, my lady and my wife.

JULIET.

That may be, sir, when I may be a wife.

PARIS.

That may be, must be, love, on Thursday next.

JULIET.

What must be shall be.

PARIS.

Come you to make confession to this father ?

JULIET.

To answer that I should confess to you.

ROMEO *and* JULIET

PARIS.

Poor soul, thy face is much abused with tears.

JULIET.

The tears have got small victory by that;
For it was bad enough before their spite.

PARIS.

Thy face is mine and thou hast slandered it.

JULIET.

It may be so, for it is not mine own.
Are you at leisure, holy father, now,
Or shall I come to you at evening mass?

FRIAR LAURENCE.

My leisure serves me, pensive daughter, now.
My lord, we must entreat the time alone.

PARIS.

[JULIET *crosses to* R.   PARIS *goes to her* L.
God shield I should disturb devotion!
Juliet, on Thursday early will I rouse ye:
Till then, adieu, and keep this holy kiss.

[*Exit through gate* L. C.
[FRIAR LAURENCE *comes to* JULIET *to support her*.

JULIET.

O, shut the door! [R. *up to chair*.] and when thou hast done so,
Come weep with me; past hope, past cure, past help!

[*In chair* R. C.

91

ROMEO *and* JULIET

FRIAR LAURENCE.
[Having closed door, returns to JULIET.
Ah, Juliet, I already know thy grief.

JULIET.
Tell me not, Friar, that thou hear'st of this,
Unless thou tell me how I may prevent it :
If in thy wisdom thou canst give no help,
Do thou but call my resolution wise,
And with this knife I 'll help it presently.
God join'd my heart and Romeo's, thou our hands ;
And ere this hand, by thee to Romeo seal'd,
Shall be the label to another deed,
Or my true heart with treacherous revolt
Turn to another, this shall slay them both ;
Therefore, out of thy long-experienc'd time,
Give me some present counsel ; or, behold,
'Twixt my extremes and me this bloody knife
Shall play the umpire.
Be not so long to speak ; I long to die,
If what thou speak'st speak not of remedy.

FRIAR LAURENCE.
Hold, daughter ! I do spy a kind of hope,
Which craves as desperate an execution
As that is desperate which we would prevent.
If, rather than to marry County Paris,
Thou hast the strength of will to slay thyself,
Then is it likely thou wilt undertake
A thing like death to chide away this shame ;
And, if thou dar'st, I 'll give thee remedy.

92

ROMEO *and* JULIET

JULIET.

O, bid me leap, rather than marry Paris,
From off the battlements of yonder tower ;
Or bid me go into a new-made grave
And hide me with a dead man in his shroud ;
Things that, to hear them told, have made me tremble ;
And I will do it without fear or doubt,
To live an unstain'd wife to my sweet love.

FRIAR LAURENCE.

Hold, then ; go home, be merry, give consent
To marry Paris. [*Getting vial from cabinet at upper end of
desk. Down L. of* JULIET.] Wednesday is to-morrow ;
To-morrow night look that thou lie alone ;
Let not thy nurse lie with thee in thy chamber.
Take out this vial, being then in bed,
And this distilled liquor drink thou off ;
When presently through all thy veins shall run
A cold and drowsy humor, for no pulse
Shall keep his native progress, but surcease.
No warmth, no breath, shall testify thou livest ;
And in this borrowed likeness of shrunk death
Thou shalt continue two and forty hours,
And then awake as from a pleasant sleep.
Now, when the bridegroom in the morning comes
To rouse thee from thy bed, there art thou dead :
Then, as the manner of our country is,
In thy best robes uncover'd on the bier
Thou shalt be borne to that same ancient vault
Where all the kindred of the Capulets lie.

ROMEO *and* JULIET

In the meantime, against thou shalt awake,
Shall Romeo by my letters know our drift,
And hither shall he come ; and he and I
Will watch thy waking, and that very night
Shall Romeo bear thee hence to Mantua.
And this shall free thee from this present shame,
If no inconstant toy nor womanish fear
Abate thy valour in the acting it.

JULIET.

[*Rises.*]   Give me, give me !   O, tell me not of fear !

FRIAR LAURENCE.

Hold ; get you gone, be strong and prosperous
In this resolve :   I 'll send a friar with speed
To Mantua, with my letters to thy lord.

JULIET.

Love give me strength ! and strength shall help afford.
Farewell, dear father !

[*Crosses to him and exit through gate L. C.*

SCENE III.—*Tuesday evening.*   NURSE *and* CAPULET *discovered,*
followed by LADY CAPULET, *who enters L.*

CAPULET.

What, is my daughter gone to Friar Laurence ?

NURSE.

Ay, forsooth.

CAPULET.

Well, he may chance to do some good on her ;
A peevish, self-will'd simpleness it is.

[LADY CAPULET *seated L. C.*

94

ROMEO *and* JULIET

NURSE.

See ! here she comes from shrift, with merry look.

[*Enter* JULIET, *L. 1 E., bows to* LADY CAPULET, *goes to her father; low courtsey.*

CAPULET.

How, now, my headstrong ! Where have you been gadding ?

JULIET.

Where I have learned me to repent the sin
Of disobedient opposition
To you and your behests, and am enjoin'd
By holy Laurence to fall prostrate here,
And beg your pardon. Pardon I beseech you !
Henceforward I am ever rul'd by you.

CAPULET.

[*To* LADY CAPULET, *who rises.*] Send for the County ; go tell
   him of this.
I 'll have this knot knit up to-morrow morning.
Now, afore God ! this reverend holy friar,
All our whole city is much bound to him.

JULIET.

[*To* NURSE, *R. of her.*] Nurse, will you go with me into
   my closet,
To help me sort such needful ornaments
As you think fit to furnish me to-morrow ?

LADY CAPULET.

No, not till Thursday ; there is time enough.

95

ROMEO *and* JULIET

CAPULET.

Go, nurse, go with her; we'll to church to-morrow.

[*Exeunt* NURSE *and* JULIET, *L.*

LADY CAPULET.

We shall be short in our provision;
'Tis now near night.

CAPULET.

[*Near door, L. 1 E.*] Tush, I will stir about,
And all things shall be well, I warrant thee, wife.
Go thou to Juliet, help to deck up her;
I'll not to bed to-night; let me alone.
I'll play the housewife for this once. [*Exeunt L. 1 E.*
[*Re-enter* JULIET *and* NURSE, *C. from L.*

JULIET.

[*Down R. C.*] Ay, those attires are best; but, gentle nurse,
I pray thee, leave me to myself to-night;
[*Nurse closes curtains of window, R.*
For I have need of many orisons
To move the heavens to smile upon my state,
Which, well thou know'st, is cross and full of sin.
[*Re-enter* LADY CAPULET, *L. 1 E.*

LADY CAPULET.

What, are you busy, ho? Need you my help?

JULIET.

No, madam; we have cull'd such necessaries
As are behoveful for our state to-morrow;
So please you, let me now be left alone,

And let the nurse this night sit up with you ;
For, I am sure, you have your hands full all
In this so sudden business.

LADY CAPULET.

[*Goes to* JULIET, *C., giving her a cold kiss on her forehead.*
Good night ;
Get thee to bed and rest, for thou hast need.
[*Exeunt* LADY CAPULET *and* NURSE, *L. 1 E.*

JULIET.

[*C.*]   Farewell !   God knows when we shall meet again.
I have a faint cold fear thrills through my veins,
That almost freezes up the heat of life ;
I 'll call them back again to comfort me.   [*Going to door.*
Nurse !—What should she do here ?
My dismal scene I needs must act alone.—
Come, vial.   [*To table, L. C.*
What if this mixture do not work at all ?
Shall I be married, then, to-morrow morning ?
No, no !   This shall forbid it.—Lie thou there.
                     [*Laying down a dagger on table.*
What if it be a poison, which the friar
Subtly hath minister'd to have me dead,
Lest in this marriage he should be dishonor'd,
Because he married me before to Romeo ?
I fear it is ; and yet, methinks, it should not,
For he hath still been tried a holy man.
How if, when I am laid into the tomb,
I wake before the time that Romeo
Come to redeem me ?   There 's a fearful point !

97

Shall I not then be stifled in the vault,
To whose foul mouth no healthsome air breathes in,
And there die strangled ere my Romeo comes?
Or, if I live, is it not very like,
The horrible conceit of death and night,
Together with the terror of the place,
Where for these many hundred years the bones
Of all my buried ancestors are pack'd;
Where bloody Tybalt, yet but green in earth,
Lies festering in his shroud; where, as they say,
At some hours in the night spirits resort;—
Alack, alack, is it not like that I,
So early waking, what with loathsome smells
And shrieks like mandrakes' torn out of the earth,
That living mortals hearing them run mad.
O, if I wake, shall I not be distraught,
Environed with all these hideous fears,
And madly play with my forefathers' joints;
And pluck the mangled Tybalt from his shroud;
And, in this rage, with some great kinsman's bone,
As with a club, dash out my desperate brains?
O, look! methinks I see my cousin's ghost
Seeking out Romeo;—Stay, Tybalt, stay!—

                         [Goes to window, R.

Romeo, I come! This do I drink to thee.

                         [She falls on the stage, C.

ACT V

SCENE I.—*Mantua.* *A Street.* *Door L. F.* *Wednesday Evening.* *Stone seat R. C.*

[*Enter* ROMEO *R. 1 E.*

ROMEO.

F I MAY trust the flattering truth of sleep,
My dreams presage some joyful news at hand.
My bosom's lord sits lightly in his throne ;
And all this day an unaccustom'd spirit
Lifts me above the ground with cheerful
    thoughts.
    I dreamt my lady came and found me dead,
And breath'd such life with kisses in my lips,
That I reviv'd, and was an emperor.
Ah me ! how sweet is love itself possess'd,
When but love's shadows are so rich in joy !
News from Verona !   [*Enter* BALTHASAR, *L. 1 E.*
        How now, Balthasar !
Dost thou not bring me letters from the friar ?
How doth my lady ? Is my father well ?
How fares my Juliet ? that I ask again ;
For nothing can be ill, if she be well.

99

ROMEO *and* JULIET

In what I farther shall intend to do,
By heaven, I will tear thee joint by joint
And strew this hungry churchyard with thy limbs.

BALTHASAR.

I will be gone, sir, and not trouble you.

ROMEO.

So shalt thou show me friendship.   Take thou that:

> [*Gives him a purse.*

Live and be prosperous ; and farewell, good fellow.

> [*Turns away.*

BALTHASAR.

[*Aside.*]   For all this same I 'll hide me here about.
His looks I fear, and his intents I doubt.   [*Exit R. 1 E.*

ROMEO.

[*Forcing open tomb.*]   Thou detestable maw, thou womb of death,

Gorged with the dearest morsel of the earth,
Thus I enforce thy rotten jaws to open,
And in despite I 'll cram thee with more food.   [*Opens tomb.*

PARIS.

[*Enters L. 1 E.   Advancing.*]   Stop thy unhallow'd toil, vile Montague !

Can vengeance be pursued further than death ?
Condemned villain, I do apprehend thee :
Obey, and go with me; for thou must die.

ROMEO.

I must indeed, and therefore came I hither.
Good gentle youth, tempt not a desperate man ;

ROMEO *and* JULIET

Let 's see for means.   O mischief, thou art swift
To enter in the thoughts of desperate men !
I do remember an apothecary,—
And hereabouts he dwells,—which late I noted
In tatter'd weeds, with overwhelming brows,
Culling of simples ; meagre were his looks,
Sharp misery had worn him to the bones ;
Noting this penury, to myself I said,
An if a man did need a poison now,
Whose sale is present death in Mantua,
Here lives a catiff wretch would sell it him.
O, this same thought did but forerun my need,
And this same needy man must sell it me !
As I remember, this should be the house.
Being holiday, the beggar's shop is shut.
What, ho ! apothecary ?   [*Knocks at door.*

APOTHECARY.

[*In doorway.*]   Who calls so loud ?

ROMEO.

Come hither, man. [*Enter* APOTHECARY.] I see that thou art
poor:
　　Hold, there is forty ducats ; let me have
　　A dram of poison, such soon-speeding gear
　　As will disperse itself through all the veins
　　That the life-weary taker may fall dead.

APOTHECARY.

Such mortal drugs I have ; but Mantua's law
Is death to any he that utters them.

101

ROMEO *and* JULIET

ROMEO.

Art thou so bare and full of wretchedness,
And fear'st to die ? famine is in thy cheeks ;
Need and oppression starveth in thine eyes ;
Contempt and beggary hang upon thy back.
The world is not thy friend, nor the world's law ;
The world affords no law to make thee rich ;
Then be not poor, but break it, and take this.

APOTHECARY.

My poverty, but not my will, consents.

ROMEO.

I pay thy poverty and not thy will.

[APOTHECARY *exit and re-enters.*

APOTHECARY.

Put this in any liquid thing you will,
And drink it off ; and, if you had the strength
Of twenty men, it would dispatch you straight.

ROMEO.

There is thy gold, worse poison to men's souls,
Doing more murthers in this loathsome world,
Than these poor compounds that thou mayst not sell :
I sell thee poison, thou hast sold me none.

[APOTHECARY *moves away.*

Farewell ; buy food, and get thyself in flesh.

[*Exit* APOTHECARY.

Come, cordial and not poison, go with me
To Juliet's grave ; for there must I use thee.

[*Exit R. 1 E.*

102

ROMEO *and* JULIET

SCENE II.—*A Churchyard; in it a tomb belonging to the* CAPU-
LETS. *Wednesday, near midnight.*
[*Enter* FRIAR LAURENCE R. *1* E., *goes toward tomb,* L. C.

FRIAR JOHN.

[*Within.*]   Holy Franciscan friar ! brother, ho !
                    [FRIAR LAURENCE *stops and turns.*
                              [*Enter* FRIAR JOHN R. *1* E.

FRIAR LAURENCE.

This same should be the voice of Friar John.
Welcome from Mantua ; what says Romeo ?
Or, if his mind be writ, give me his letter.

FRIAR JOHN.

Going to find a bare-foot brother out,
One of our order, to associate me,
Here in this city visiting the sick,
And finding him,—the searchers of the town,
Suspecting that we both were in a house
Where the infectious pestilence did reign,
Seal'd up the doors, and would not let us forth ;
So that my speed to Mantua there was stay'd.

FRIAR LAURENCE.

Who bare my letter, then, to Romeo ?

FRIAR JOHN.

I could not send it,—here it is again,—
Nor get a messenger to bring it thee,
So fearful were they of infection.

103

ROMEO *and* JULIET

FRIAR LAURENCE.

Unhappy fortune ! by my brotherhood,
The letter was not nice, but full of charge
Of dear import, and the neglecting it
May do much danger.   Friar John, go hence ;
Get me an iron crow, and bring it straight
Unto my cell.

FRIAR JOHN.

Brother, I 'll go and bring it thee.   [*Exit R. 1 E.*

FRIAR LAURENCE.

Within this three hours will fair Juliet wake.
She will beshrew me much that Romeo
Hath had no notice of these accidents.
But I will write again to Mantua,
And keep her at my cell till Romeo come :
Poor living corpse, closed in a dead man's tomb !

                    [*Exit R. 1 E.*
        [*Enter* PARIS, *and his Page bearing flowers and a torch,*
        L. 1 E.

PARIS.

Give me thy torch, boy; hence, and stand aloof:
Yet put it out, for I would not be seen.
Under yond yew-trees lay thee all along,   [*Pointing off R.*
Holding thine ear close to the hollow ground ;
So shall no foot upon the churchyard tread,
Being loose, unfirm, with digging up of graves,
But thou shalt hear it : whistle then to me,
As signal that thou hear'st something approach.
Give me those flowers.   Do as I bid thee, go.

                [*Takes flowers and turns to tomb.*

104

ROMEO *and* JULIET

PAGE.

[*Crosses to R., then pauses. Aside.*]   1 am almost afraid to
stand alone
  Here in the churchyard ; yet I will adventure.   [*Exit R. 1 E.*

PARIS.

[*Before tomb.*]   Sweet flower, with flowers thy bridal bed 1
strew.
  O woe ! thy canopy is dust and stones.
  The obsequies that I for thee will keep
  Nightly shall be to strew thy grave and weep.
                              [*The Page whistles R.*
  The boy gives warning something doth approach.
  What cursed foot wanders this way to-night ?
                                    [*Retires L. 1 E.*
                [*Enter* ROMEO, *and* BALTHASAR *with a torch, mattock,*
                  etc., R. 1 E.

ROMEO.

Give me the wrenching iron.
  Hold, take this letter ; early in the morning
  See thou deliver it to my lord and father.
  Upon thy life, I charge thee,
  Whate'er thou hear'st or seest, stand all aloof,
  And do not interrupt me in my course.
  Why I descend into this bed of death
  Is partly to behold my lady's face,
  But chiefly to take thence from her dead finger
  A precious ring, a ring that I must use
  In dear employment.   Therefore hence, be gone.
  But if thou, jealous, dost return to pry

In what I farther shall intend to do,
By heaven, I will tear thee joint by joint
And strew this hungry churchyard with thy limbs.

BALTHASAR.

I will be gone, sir, and not trouble you.

ROMEO.

So shalt thou show me friendship.   Take thou that :

[Gives him a purse.

Live and be prosperous ; and farewell, good fellow.

[Turns away.

BALTHASAR.

[*Aside.*]   For all this same I 'll hide me here about.
His looks I fear, and his intents I doubt.   [*Exit R. 1 E.*

ROMEO.

[*Forcing open tomb.*]   Thou detestable maw, thou womb of
death,

Gorged with the dearest morsel of the earth,
Thus I enforce thy rotten jaws to open,
And in despite I 'll cram thee with more food.   [*Opens tomb.*

PARIS.

[*Enters L. 1 E.   Advancing.*]   Stop thy unhallow'd toil, vile
Montague !

Can vengeance be pursued further than death ?
Condemned villain, I do apprehend thee :
Obey, and go with me ; for thou must die.

ROMEO.

I must indeed, and therefore came I hither.
Good gentle youth, tempt not a desperate man ;

Fly hence and leave me : I beseech thee, youth,
Put not another sin upon my head,
By urging me to fury ; O, be gone !
By heaven, I love thee better than myself,
For I come hither arm'd against myself.
Stay not, be gone; live, and hereafter say,
A madman's mercy bade thee run away.

PARIS.

I do defy thy conjurations,
And apprehend thee for a felon here !
                              [*Advancing and seizing him.*

ROMEO.

Wilt thou provoke me ? then have at thee, boy !
               [*They fight with daggers.* ROMEO *stabs* PARIS.

PARIS.

O, I am slain ! [*Falls.*] If thou be merciful,
Open the tomb, lay me with Juliet. [*Dies.*

ROMEO.

[*Back of* PARIS.] In faith, I will.—Let me peruse this face.
Mercutio's kinsman, noble County Paris !
One writ with me in sour misfortune's book !
What said my man when my betossed soul
Did not attend him as we rode ? I think
He told me Paris should have married Juliet.
Said he not so ? Or did I dream it so ?
O, give me thy hand !
I 'll bury thee in a triumphant grave.

ROMEO *and* JULIET

SCENE III.—*Interior of the tomb.* JULIET *lying on the bier,* C.
ROMEO *discovered, bearing* PARIS'*s body. Places it up L.*
C., then goes to C., back of bier.

ROMEO.

         O my love ! my wife !
Death, that hath suck'd the honey of thy breath
Hath had no power yet upon thy beauty :
Thou art not conquer'd ; beauty's ensign yet
Is crimson in thy lips and in thy cheeks,
And death's pale flag is not advanced there.
         Ah, dear Juliet,
Why art thou so fair ?—O, here,
Will I set up my everlasting rest,
And shake the yoke of inauspicious stars
From this world-wearied flesh.—Eyes, look your last !
Arms, take your last embrace ? and, lips, O you
The doors of breath, seal with a righteous kiss
A dateless bargain to engrossing death !
Come, bitter conduct, come, unsavoury guide !
                [*Comes in front of bier.*
Thou desperate pilot, now at once run on
The dashing rocks thy sea-sick weary bark !
Here 's to my love ! [*Drinks.*] O true apothecary !
Thy drugs are quick.—Thus with a kiss I die. [*Dies.*
[*Enter* FRIAR LAURENCE, *down steps L. H., carrying a lantern.*

FRIAR LAURENCE.

Saint Francis be my speed ! how oft to-night
Have my old feet stumbled at graves !—Who 's there ?
                [*Crosses to C.*

ROMEO *and* JULIET

Romeo ! O, pale ! Who else ? What, Paris,too ? [*Goes up L. C.*
And steep'd in blood ?   Ah, what an unkind hour
Is guilty of this lamentable chance !
　　　[*Places lantern on stage by* PARIS, *and returns to* JULIET.
The lady stirs.
　　　　　　　　　　　　　　　　[JULIET *wakes.*

JULIET.

O comfortable friar !   Where is my lord ?
I do remember well where I should be,
[*Sitting up.*]   And there I am.   Where is my Romeo ?

FRIAR LAURENCE.

[*L. of* JULIET.] I hear some noise. Lady, come from that nest
Of death, contagion and unnatural sleep ;
A greater power than we can contradict
Hath twarted our intents.   Come, come away.
Thy husband in thy bosom there lies dead ;
　　　　　　　　　　[*Points to* ROMEO *in front of bier.*
And Paris too.   Come, I 'll dispose of thee
Among a sisterhood of holy nuns :
Stay not to question, for the watch is coming ;
　　　　　　　　　　　　[*Starts towards arch L. 2 E.*
Come, go, good Juliet. [*Returns to her.*] I dare no longer stay.

JULIET.

Go, get thee hence, for I will not away.
　　　　　　　　[*Exit* FRIAR LAURENCE *up stairs D. H.*
[JULIET *kisses* ROMEO.]   Thy lips are warm.
　　　　　　　　　[*Murmurs, then words, heard within.*

WATCH.

[*Within.*]   Lead, boy ; which way ?

BALTHASAR.

[*Within.*] This is the place—there, where the torch doth burn.

JULIET.

Yea, noise? then I 'll be brief.   O happy dagger !

[*Snatching* ROMEO's *dagger.*

This is thy sheath. [*Stabs herself.*] There rust, and let me die.

[*Falls on* ROMEO's *body and dies.*

[FRIAR LAURENCE *enters L. 2 and stands in archway.*

END OF THE PL·AY.

Printed in the United States
100399LV00008B/288/A

9 780548 306666